From Lover to Beloved

Experience God's hope, healing, and forgiveness after committing adultery

Brenna Naufel

COPYRIGHT

FROM LOVER TO BELOVED

earn a small commission at no cost to you.

For more information, email brenna@skippinglikeacalf.com.

www.skippinglikeacalf.com

www.fromlovertobeloved.com

ISBN: 979-8-9872979-2-6

WAIT! GET YOUR FREE WORKBOOK!

To help you go deeper together with God through this healing journey, I created a free bonus workbook that includes additional thoughts and reflection questions directly corresponding to the chapters in this book. **Visit the following link to get this free workbook now:**

www.fromlovertobeloved.com/workbook/

Dedication

To my husband, Garrett. In the midst of my greatest sin and rebellion, you chose to love me with God's heart and fight for our marriage. Without your willingness to walk through this horrendous betrayal and heartbreak, we would not be here together now nor have the beautiful children we have today. I am so incredibly thankful for your perseverance and the life that we have together! With all my heart, THANK YOU for choosing forgiveness and reconciliation.

Thank you

- My Mom – Even when I first told you of my infidelity, you encouraged me and offered hope that God would use this season of our lives for good. You have continued to be faithful in prayer over our lives, and we are so grateful!

- My Dad and Stepmom, June – You were some of the very first people we turned to as we embarked on this tumultuous journey of healing after infidelity. You embraced us and provided a safe haven for us as we worked to heal. Thank you for your love and many prayers!

- Garrett's Parents & all of our Siblings – Thank you all for loving me despite my sin, for praying for us, and for supporting us! You never turned your face from me and showered me with love and care. We are forever grateful.

- My Counselor and Spiritual Director, Kelly Wright – Kelly, you have played a pivotal role in our lives as we worked towards healing from my affair. Your lovingkindness, godly insight, and wisdom were crucial to our reconciliation and the redemption of our relationship. Garrett and I are forever grateful to you!

- Korrin Ingalls – Despite your very full life, you took me under your wing and loved me in the aftermath of my affair. You always listened to whatever I had to share with the utmost compassion. Thank you, friend!

- Our former church family, The Rock, and in memory of Pastor John Drage – As a church, you embraced us during our darkest days. You didn't shy away from me or cast me out. John, you in particular, always championed and encouraged us. We miss your infectious smile and friendship dearly, and can't wait to be reunited with you again in heaven when our time comes.

- To those who financially supported the self-publishing of this book! Evan and Katie Courtney, Vicki Ghea, Gary and Ginny Naufel, Terry and June Seboldt, Kelly and Hartley Wright, and many others! Your selflessness has made this book a reality! Thank you!

With much love, Brenna

Contents

Chapter 1

Does Your Husband Know?

Andy strolled into my office and casually plopped down in my red guest chair as if it wasn't odd he was there. He had abruptly quit the company we worked at in downtown Columbia, Missouri, without explanation a couple of weeks prior. I was puzzled as to why he now visited me.

My weekly Friday morning staff meeting was about to start, so I tried to make quick pleasantries, hoping to say goodbye and go about my day. However, my day was about to be anything but ordinary.

"Does your husband know that you slept with Trey?" Andy blurted out. I felt like I had been sucker-punched in the heart. Here I was, finally coming face-to-face with the sin that had enslaved me for the past five years.

—— *ele* ——

I met my husband, Garrett, twelve years before this fateful day at a Christian college leadership training program held over the summer in Myrtle Beach, South Carolina. Garrett arrived several days late due to a friend's wedding, so instead of the group he was supposed to be housed with, he lived with the guys from the University of Texas (UT). I had just moved to Austin, Texas to be with this amazing group of students I had met the summer before attending the same program, so I lived with the girls.

I went into that summer with my eyes still set on my ex-boyfriend, Chris. We had broken up just a couple of months before the summer, and he, too, lived with the guys from UT. However, God quickly got my attention through a sermon about wiping the slate of our lives clean so He could write His story for us. In particular, I felt like clearing the board related to relationships was precisely what God wanted me to do. I was tired of manipulating and exhausted from searching for the "right guy." In my haste and desire for a relationship, I didn't want to settle for less than what God knew was best for me.

So, I let it all go. I wholeheartedly told the Lord that I was all His. My relationships were His. And most of all, I didn't want to date anyone ever again unless they intended to marry me. Extreme, perhaps, but in every relationship before, I had quickly cast God aside in pursuit of guys. I had even dated two guys who wanted to marry me but didn't even believe God existed.

Enter Garrett. My heart's first response to Garrett after chatting with him one night was that he was someone I simply wanted to encourage. There were no ulterior motives, no agenda. I desired to love him as Christ loves him and to encourage him daily. I began writing him notes of encouragement, and he soon returned the favor.

After just three short weeks, I felt God whispering to my heart that this would be the guy I would marry. "What, God? I just told you I don't want to be doing this right now. Don't you remember?" Yet, day after day, I continued to feel God work on my heart and affirm that Garrett was the guy.

Meanwhile, God moved in Garrett's heart. Garrett was set to attend Colorado State University (CSU) in the fall with a full ride to pursue his doctorate. Yet halfway through the summer, he fell in love with the Texas students, just as I had the summer before, and he wanted to pursue ministry. He wasn't thinking about me as a potential romantic partner at all during this time so even though I began to believe he was "the right guy," I steered clear of giving any opinions as to what he should or shouldn't do. And, again, I didn't want to manipulate the situation.

After speaking to some friends one night about trying to decide whether or not to move to Texas, Garrett became livid as they asked if he was just thinking about moving there because of his friendship with me. As he recounted the story to me while we strolled along the sandy beach at twilight, he blurted out, "I mean, I would never date you or marry you!"

Tears trickled down my face like the ocean waves that lapped against the shore. Garrett, completely off-guard, quickly stammered, "I mean, if I were able to be with someone who is even a drop in the bucket compared to you, I would be blessed." Good recovery, buddy.

God continued to impress upon my heart daily that Garrett was the one. In one ridiculous moment of being extra clear, Garrett and I sat by each other just ONE time the entire summer out of twenty church services. And in the middle of a message about reaching the world with the gospel, the pastor went on a huge tangent and said, "I mean, for some of you, the person you are sitting next to is the person you are going to marry!" Nice, God. I get it.

Garrett chose to give up the full ride at CSU to move to Texas to pursue ministry, and soon after that, he began to think about me as a potential wife. As we continued to write to each other and spend more time together, we agreed we needed to chat. So, we took a day apart to fast, pray, seek counsel, and come back together on that ever-fateful beach.

Just eight short weeks after we had met, Garrett asked me, "So, what do you think?"

I told him, "I really want to date you, but not unless you intend to marry me."

He quickly replied, "I do want to marry you," and told me how he wanted to be by my side to pursue God and people for His kingdom.

Just a month after that, he moved to Texas and officially proposed. I never once doubted that out of all the people in the world, Garrett was whom God chose for me and me for him. There were things I didn't know I wanted or needed that God knew Garrett would provide. This love was truly a patient love—a kind of love unlike any other I had experienced in my twenty-one years of life.

ell

Now, here I was, being confronted about my horrendous sin. I was shocked. I vehemently denied Andy's allegations, even though they were entirely true. And no, Garrett did not know I had an affair with Trey. I fought back the tears as my heart raced, knowing everything was about to change. I felt embarrassed. I felt scared—no, terrified. I wanted to throw up. Finally, Andy left, stating that Garrett had the right to know.

I sat pale-faced in my office for a while, missing most of the staff meeting, continuing to work, and pretending everything was okay. I couldn't concentrate on anything. Emotions of every kind flooded my soul, and it was all I could do to fight back the tears that longed to pour out of my aching heart. My eyes continuously monitored the clock, agonizing over every excruciating minute until my lunch break arrived so I could just get away.

When my break finally came, I ran to my car. I quickly drove to a nearby park, making every effort to stay focused on the road through the tears that clouded my vision. I parked in an empty parking space and simply broke down.

For the next hour, I sat in my car and wept. Tears flooded my face and drenched my shirt as I started to process all that was about to happen. A myriad of emotions rose within me as I sat alone in that car—ashamed, horrified, and angry. Angry at Trey for digging his manipulative hooks in me, keeping me close by for his sexual convenience. Furious with myself for ever allowing this sin into my life and for letting it reign there for so long.

My heart broke as I grieved all I had done and all that was to come. I cried out to the God I had forsaken for so long, asking Him what to do. I was faced with the reality of the tapestry of hurt I had weaved that would cover Garrett's heart and rip our lives apart. I begged God to tell me if there was any way for me to repent but not have to confess to Garrett. I didn't want to crush his heart and soul. Yet, the damage was already done. "But Lord," I humbly said, "I will do whatever you ask."

The weekend couldn't come fast enough as I tried to determine my next steps. To complicate matters, I was our primary source of income and health insurance, and I knew I would have to leave my job immediately since I worked with Trey. Garrett was on staff with a college ministry and didn't make much money; that had always been our choice and sacrifice. So, not only was I faced with having to confess this wretched affair, but I was also faced with losing our main source of income and livelihood.

That Saturday, my time was divided between updating my resume, searching for new jobs, and seeking opinions online as to whether or not to tell your spouse about an affair. It was not hard to come by a plethora of opinions about confession in this realm.

Trey was in one ear, along with many others in various forums, saying, "Don't tell. You don't want to go through that heartache and hurt your spouse. They don't need to know." Yet, I found myself reeling at those words of "advice." They made me so incredibly angry. How can anyone say your spouse doesn't need to know? I knew deep in my heart that *telling* my husband what I had done wasn't what would hurt him. Instead, *doing* what I had already done would hurt him, and I could never take it back.

I didn't want to tell Garrett because I didn't know what would happen. I was terrified. Would he slip into a state of depression and never get out? Would he hurt himself? Would he leave me and hate me for as long as he lived? I had so many questions and absolutely no answers.

But, Andy was right. Garrett had the right to know. And I believed in my heart there was no way in the world I could genuinely repent without fully coming into the light. I would never be free from the entanglement of this sin if it were to remain hidden. After all, my deepest longing was to be fully known and fully loved by the man I had married. How could I ever be fully loved if I would not allow myself to be fully known? To be fully known, I would have to share everything about this affair and commit to being truthful and honest no matter what happened.

On Monday, I told Trey I would tell Garrett everything and quit my job. He didn't like that at all. Not only did he not want to lose me as a "friend," but also as a coworker. He asked if anything at all would make me change my mind. I emphatically said, "No."

He then pleaded with me to think of him and at least wait until the divorce with his wife was final, which would be a few months down the road. I thought *this is the most selfish thing I have ever heard. I put everything in jeopardy for this man? How ridiculous!* It seemed like the devil himself was whispering lies, trying to deceive my heart once again. Trey wasn't concerned about Garrett or my marriage—he was only worried about his wife learning of his infidelity, his image, and most likely his money.

I was adamant about doing what was right, and a big part of me felt relieved it would finally be over. I had tried so many times to end the affair, but Satan had me by the bit in my mouth. I did not confess my sin to others and lived in darkness. I made the mistake of staying in my job and not getting as far away from Trey as possible. I was not going to make any of those mistakes again. And Trey knew me well enough to know he couldn't change my mind.

While I knew I didn't want to wait all summer to tell Garrett to appease Trey in any way, I also didn't know when to confess to him. Our pastors would soon leave for the entire summer. That following weekend I was supposed to go to Italy for a week with my mom. And I was still concerned about the job situation. Several days passed as I tried to pull it all together.

However, I would have no more time. The Wednesday after being confronted, Garrett called me at work and asked me to come home as soon as possible. I hung up the phone, quickly packed my things, and drove the ten minutes to our house. Hoping this wasn't going to be what I, deep down in my heart, thought it was, I pulled into the garage and sheepishly walked into the living room where Garrett waited.

He was so sweet and sincere. He sat me down on the couch and took my hand. I braced myself as best as I could. Then, with a cautious voice and wondering eyes, he said, "Brenna, I'm sorry, but I have to ask you a question."

He apologized to me for having to ask what seemed like such an absurd question, an impossible question—one to which he surely knew the answer. He didn't want to accuse me of something I certainly did not do.

"Andy called me today and told me that you had slept with Trey...is it true?"

Chapter 2

Naked on the Battlefield

John, one of our pastors, came over as soon as he got the call from Garrett. When he arrived, he gave us both big hugs, and we all sat in our living room. He proceeded to ask me more questions.

"How long did the affair go on?"

I could barely whisper the answer. "Almost five years."

"Is there anything else you need to tell us?"

Unfortunately, yes, there was. There was a lot to tell. I swallowed my pride and came clean about everything.

There were also three other men I had brief physical encounters with (but didn't have sex with) within the past five years. I could barely formulate words to communicate the atrocities I had committed. Bluntly verbalizing my actions to my husband and pastor made me sick. Every word pierced an arrow straight into my beloved husband's heart. I hated what I had done to him and what I was doing to him now.

I never set out to have an affair and cheat on my husband. As I walked down the aisle eleven years ago and exchanged vows with my husband-to-be, I didn't hatch a grand master plan to cheat on him and shatter his heart. Instead, I made vows to forsake all others and to be faithful to him and him only, and I wholeheartedly meant them. Every part of me believed Garrett was the best man in the world to be my husband. Plus, God brought us together.

I didn't want to leave Garrett, and I didn't want to hurt him. Beneath all the chains of sin that entangled me, I still knew Garrett was whom I loved and who truly loved me. Yet, for some reason, I chose to rebel against God and sin against Him, and my husband, in the most heinous way. I had frivolously cast Garrett's heart aside.

How does one go from being a loving Christian wife married to a wonderful man in ministry to going completely off the deep end in just six short years of marriage? Let's rewind a bit.

During our engagement and the first few years of our marriage, Garrett and I continued living in Austin, Texas with the beautiful group of friends we bonded with from our summers in Myrtle Beach, South Carolina. I loved this group of college students and young professionals who truly did all aspects of life together—serving, living, eating, working, and playing. Most importantly, we all loved the Lord and spurred one another on. It was a sweet phase of life.

About three-and-a-half years into our marriage, Garrett was approved to go on staff with a missions organization for college ministry. However, when it came time to decide where to serve in ministry, we chose Columbia, Missouri, at the University of Missouri, instead of staying in Austin.

The initial move to Columbia wasn't to get involved with the new church on campus but rather to begin the arduous process of raising financial support. This process entailed Garrett calling hundreds of people to share about the ministry and seek financial support so that he could serve college students full-time. He had countless meetings with people we knew as well as people we had never met before.

It was an incredibly lonely season of life. At the time, we didn't realize just how difficult it would be to leave the community of friends we had in Austin. I personally felt a connection and purpose with this group of people I never had before. Having gone to two junior high schools and four different high schools, friendships and a sense of community did not come easy for me. Having lived in Austin for just five years, it was the longest time I had lived in any one place in my entire life. The church group in Austin finally felt like home and leaving took a significant toll on my heart.

On top of that, I felt an emotional distance from Garrett that I could not explain. I began to feel there was something in between him and God as well as him and me. I just had no idea what it was at the time.

Not long after we moved, I stopped spending time with the Lord. I wasn't regularly in His Word. Somewhere in the recesses of my mind, I held the false belief I could coast by on my previous experiences with God. After all, I had a pretty good foundation, and everything would be fine, right? What's the big deal? We would be plugged into a church soon, and I could experience Jesus through that avenue.

Here's the thing. We NEED our daily bread, God's Word, to sustain us:

But He answered and said, "It is written, 'Man shall not live on bread alone, but on every word that proceeds out of the mouth of God." (Matthew 4:4, NKJV)

"I am the living bread that came down from heaven. Whoever eats this bread will live forever. This bread is my flesh, which I will give for the life of the world." (John 6:51, NIV)

Jesus said to them, "I am the bread of life; he who comes to Me will not hunger, and he who believes in Me will never thirst." (John 6:35, ESV)

I was slowly starving myself. But, instead of partaking in the only bread that satisfies, I opened myself up to consuming other things to quench my hunger and thirst.

Instead of believing the truth about God's pursuit of me, I began to allow my mind to wander with fantasies about other men pursuing me. In my mind, it was never about engaging in any kind of physical activity, but, honestly, about being pursued. I wanted to be wanted. Even in my fantasies, I would stop it short of anything "actually happening."

Yet, those fantasies eventually led to real-life flirtations. After just a couple of interactions, Trey flirted with me through subtle gestures such as tapping his finger on my knee and a look in his eye. After knowing him for several years, I saw him use the same method on other women. Yet, I fell for it at the time. It made me feel seen. Special. Desirable.

I had purposefully met Trey with hopes of getting a foot in the door at the company where he worked. My honest intent was to network, to get a chance to do something I thought I would enjoy and be good at in my career. Well, I wound up getting my foot in the door where he worked, but certainly never in the way I intended.

Prior to working with Trey, I allowed myself to be alone with him, and he took the opportunity to kiss me. That kiss crossed "the line" that sent me tumbling out of control, yet I still chose to take a position at the company where he worked. I didn't turn and run away. Before that kiss, I was inching toward "the line," never believing I would ever cross it. Yet, now that I had crossed it, all broke loose and led to a five-year-long affair.

However, God doesn't call us to not cross a line that we, in our own wisdom, have drawn in the sand. He calls us to run in the opposite direction of the line and to run toward Him, toward holiness. *We* draw the line, deceiving ourselves that we are doing okay in the holiness department if we just don't cross that line. Oftentimes, when that line is crossed, or even as we get dangerously close to it, we draw another line a bit further out, telling ourselves, "Okay, as long as I don't cross *this* line, I will be okay."

You see, friend, I was not running in the right direction. I had laid down my armor and started looking to other things to satisfy my aching heart. And just because I naively laid down my armor doesn't mean I was no longer in battle! Instead, it left me 100% buck naked on the battlefield and made me an easy target for the enemy.

> Therefore put on the full armor of God, so that when the day of evil comes, you may be able to stand your ground, and after you have done everything, to stand. Stand firm then, with the belt of truth buckled around your waist, with the breastplate of righteousness in place, and with your feet fitted with the readiness that comes from the gospel of

peace. In addition to all this, take up the shield of faith, with which you can extinguish all the flaming arrows of the evil one. Take the helmet of salvation and the sword of the Spirit, which is the word of God. (Ephesians 6:13-17, NIV)

When is the day of evil? It's *any moment* of spiritual attack which could come at *any time*. So, even though I had previously put on the armor of God, I had stopped putting it on by neglecting time in God's Word and not fixing my mind on things above. As a result, I was left completely exposed, ready for the enemy to pounce.

Be sober-minded; be watchful. Your adversary the devil prowls around like a roaring lion, seeking someone to devour. (1 Peter 5:8, ESV)

The armor of God is vital to our survival and determines whether we live in freedom or captivity. Unfortunately, I had laid down the breastplate of righteousness, leaving my heart, the most vulnerable part of me, completely exposed. I ignored the wise counsel we are offered in Proverbs 4:23 (NIV), "Above all else, guard your heart, for everything you do flows from it." I definitely do not do that.

I laid down the belt of truth and my shield of faith. I believed the enemy's flaming arrows, the lies that pierced my heart to its core:

This is just who you are.
God will never take you back.
You have messed up too much for too long.
There is no forgiveness for you.
You are hopeless.

When I stopped spending time in the Word, I laid down my only weapon, the sword of the Spirit. The most powerful weapon was at my disposal, and I had tossed it aside.

> For the word of God is alive and powerful. It is sharper than the sharpest two-edged sword, cutting between soul and spirit, between joint and marrow. It exposes our innermost thoughts and desires. (Hebrews 4:12, NLT)

That helmet of salvation? There was nothing now protecting my mind. My feet were no longer fitted with the readiness that comes from the gospel of peace but were sunk deep in muck and mire.

And here's the thing. It's so easy to lay down the armor, to forget that not only are we in a full-blown war but we are actively hunted. Life gets busy. We think we're doing okay and we've got this. We're above doing XYZ. We would never do [fill in the blank].

That's what I believed. After all, my dad had an affair when I was eight years old, leading to my parents' divorce. It broke our family apart. *I* would *never* do such a thing.

I am not here to say, "Satan made me do it." But, I am here to say we have a very real and ruthless enemy that wants nothing more than to entangle us in sin and to break up what God has put together.

So, when Trey kissed me in real life and I thought I would turn away, I didn't. Why? There just simply isn't a good answer to that question, certainly not an excusable one. Nothing could ever justify what I did, nor do I blame anyone or anything else for my actions.

I can tell you that I wasn't looking to God for fulfillment and reassurance of my identity in Him. I can tell you that due to Trey's senior-level position in the company there was a part of me that felt taken care of and special. And I would be remiss and not fully honest if I didn't acknowledge that it *felt good* to feel wanted, pursued, and desirable.

After all, if sin felt 100% terrible all of the time, would we struggle with it so much? I had created a hole in my heart that only God could fill. And God is the *only* one who can truly fill it. Yet, in my human nature, I sought so many other things to fill that void.

While I often felt wanted and desirable in my affair, there were many times when I also felt incredibly used—less than, unknown, just another body to be had. I hated what I was doing. I hated constantly telling lies and living in fear. It brought on another whole world of hurt to my heart. Sin has significant consequences.

I can relate to the Apostle Paul when he says, "I don't really understand myself, for I want to do what is right, but I don't do it. Instead, I do what I hate." (Romans 7:15, NLV) Does that feel familiar?

Yet, I continued to attempt to fill that void with the affair. Others may try to fill the void with pornography, alcohol, drugs, shopping, etc. While those things seem to temporarily satisfy us, we are still left with a void. We return to those things to get that sense of temporary satisfaction. And after a short while, we feel empty and unsatisfied. We find ourselves in a vicious cycle, making it incredibly difficult to break free. As it says in Proverbs 26:11, NLT, "As a dog returns to its vomit, so a fool repeats his foolishness."

Isaiah sums up this cycle perfectly as well. "The poor, deluded fool feeds on ashes. He trusts something that can't help him at all. Yet he cannot bring himself to ask, 'Is this idol that I'm holding in my hand a lie?'" (Isaiah 44:20, NLT)

We are never truly satisfied or at peace. We continue to feed on ashes and refuse to recognize we are desperately clinging to a lie. We keep doing the same thing and even intensify our efforts, thinking more of the bad medicine will surely be the cure. This cycle gave Satan a foothold in my life; my heart and mind had truly become his playground. I was 100% his prisoner, enslaved to sin.

In the book *Captivating*, John and Stasi Eldredge address this vicious cycle and the yearnings of the heart:

> When we camp our hearts in self-doubt, condemning thoughts, or even shame because those emotions have become familiar and comfortable, we are faithlessly indulging rather than allowing our deep ache

to draw us to God. Unfortunately, our indulgences make us feel better...for a while. They seem to "work"; but really only increase our need to indulge again. This is the nightmare of addiction. But it goes beyond "drugs." We give our hearts to all sorts of other "lovers" that demand our attention, demand we indulge again. We taste something that we think is good, our longings cease to ache, for a minute, but later we find ourselves empty once more, needing to be filled again and again.[1]

Here's the good news! Although Satan relentlessly does *everything* he can to keep us in prison to our sins, Jesus paid our ransom in full and nothing else is required for our freedom!

Paul tells us in Galatians 5:1, NIV, "It is for freedom that Christ has set us free. Stand firm, then, and do not let yourselves be burdened again by a yoke of slavery."

And not only have we been set free, but when we have a relationship with Jesus Christ, we also have access to the full armor of God and can break this cycle. Yet, as Paul states, we must actively put it on! And once we put it on, we have to keep it on. We're in a constant battle with the enemy over our hearts, and he delights in nothing more than piercing us with his lies and taking us captive.

I was so blind while I continued the affair that I failed to recognize I was at war. I thought all was lost and I could not be rescued.

As long as you draw breath, it is never too late to call out to the Lord with confession, to turn away from sin and Satan's lies, and to put the armor on! And then, when spiritual attacks are thrown your way, or life circumstances seem hopeless, you will stand firm!

Chapter 3

Enslaved to Sin

Bondage. Prison. Pit of despair. Mud and mire.

These are just a few of the words used in the Bible to describe being stuck in sin. And if you have been there, drowning in the cesspool of sin, you know these words can't even begin to describe the utter hardness of heart and death that have occurred within you.

Beyond the consequences of my sin with my marriage, our church, and loved ones, it took a heavy toll on me as well. There were times after I had been with Trey when I would simply cry. I didn't want to be doing what I was doing, yet I kept doing it. I could *feel* the Holy Spirit grieve within me.

I could relate to David when he writes, "When I kept silent, my bones wasted away through my groaning all day long. For day and night your hand was heavy upon me; my strength was sapped as in the heat of summer." (Psalms 32:3-4, NIV) Yep, that was me.

I had multiple panic attacks (something I had never struggled with previously), my nerves were shot, and I was diagnosed with neuropathy. I even started taking sleep medication. But, most alarming was when nearly every night I continued in my sin, I felt spiritually attacked as I went to sleep. At the time, I was so incredibly deceived that I didn't fully recognize it.

As I would start to drift off, I felt as though I was being held down and my voice was taken from me. In my spirit, I would try to get out of bed and crawl to our bedroom door to call for Garrett, but I couldn't do it. With me working a regular daytime job and Garrett being in college ministry, I often went to bed alone.

Everything in me would try to call his name, but nothing would come out, and he would never hear me or know of my struggle. I felt terrified and alone. Often, this process would repeat itself several times a night.

Sadly enough, once I finally confessed the affair and shared this experience with Garrett, he affirmed there were times he would come to bed later in the evening and felt an evil presence in the corner of the room. Yet, he never said anything about it either. How incredibly sad that we were so distant from one another. This went on for five years!

—— *ele* ——

One of the most beautiful analogies God gave me about being enslaved to sin came a few months after my confession. Even though Garrett was on sabbatical for six months, we still attended the church's staff retreat for several days in Estes Park, Colorado. I was excited to go on a hike to get some time with the Lord while Garrett was in meetings. God taught me several things on this particular hike that I will share throughout this book, but here is the first.

I chose to hike a route that passed by the livery where the horses were kept. Now, in my mind, we're in Colorado with wide-open spaces. I envisioned horses galloping across the plains, their manes blowing in the wind, delighting in the glory, majesty, and beauty of their surroundings. And that when the horses would see me, they would come running over to me, and we would have a bonding moment. Yes, this is what I envisioned, no joke.

Needless to say, that is not what happened. Instead, as I came around a bend, I saw the first horse and wondered why the horse wasn't acknowledging me. "At least turn your head buddy and give me something here," I muttered. I felt the sting of disappointment in my heart that the God-moment I had hoped for was not going to happen.

But, as I got closer to the horse, I could see why he wasn't moving. He had a bit in his mouth and was tied very tightly to a pole in front of him. And I saw more horses, and they were all the same. Horse after horse, not even able to move their heads because they were tied so tightly to that pole. And I was livid to see them this way. *This is not what these horses were created for! This is not right!*

God gave me a different moment with Him—the one I needed most. He gently reminded me of Psalm 32:9, NIV, which says, "Do not be like the horse or the mule, which have no understanding but must be controlled by bit and bridle or they will not come to you."

God continued to speak tenderly to me, "Brenna, *you* were like this horse. I created you to run freely in my love for you, with my gentle breeze of grace running through your hair. Sin is a prison, but in me, you are free. So run in my life and freedom."

I could clearly see my past self in those horses who couldn't even turn their heads to the right or left. The yoke of slavery had burdened me. There was no freedom in that life. They were created for so much more. I was created for so much more.

Now, here's the deal. *You* were created for so much more—to live a life free from the bondage of sin, showered with grace upon grace, and for intimacy with the God of the Universe, who delights in you.

You are God's workmanship (Ephesians 2:10). And your body is the temple of God in which the Holy Spirit dwells (1 Corinthians 3:16). You need to clear the temple of what doesn't belong!

Let's read the passage in scripture about Jesus clearing the temple:

> On reaching Jerusalem, Jesus entered the temple area and began driving out those who were buying and selling there. He overturned the tables of the money changers and the benches of those selling doves, and would not allow anyone to carry merchandise through the temple courts. And as he taught them, he said, "Is it not written, 'My

house will be called a house of prayer for all nations?' But you have made it a den of robbers." (Mark 11:15-17, NIV)

This scripture had new meaning for me in the aftermath of my affair. **My body is a temple of God, but I had made it into a den of robbers.** I sold things that were not mine to sell. I exchanged what was good for something evil—God's temple had been defiled.

We must be in the light to run in His freedom and delight in His joy. And together with Jesus, we can turn over the tables, drive out what doesn't belong, and allow ourselves to be a house of prayer once again. We must grab ahold of His mighty hand that reaches down to save us, that pulls us out of the mud and mire.

He lifted me out of the slimy pit, out of the mud and mire; he set my feet on a rock and gave me a firm place to stand. (Psalm 40:2, NIV)

Yet, we allow ourselves to remain in the slimy pit with Satan's foot on our necks due to our fear, stubbornness, or pride, whatever it is. But the whole reason we are in the pit is because we, like Eve in the Garden of Eden, question God's goodness and His provision for our every need. We think He must be holding out on us, and in our hearts, we believe His commands are suffocating and don't allow for true freedom.

As a culture, our mantra is "Don't tell me what to do!" We tend to even look upon God's Word with that streak of stubbornness. **Somewhere along the way, we bought into the lie that to follow God's commands is slavery and to do whatever we want is freedom. And what a lie that is!**

> Repent, then, and turn to God, so that your sins may be wiped out, that times of refreshing may come from the Lord... (Acts 3:19, NIV)

Are you ready for a time of refreshing? To be lifted out of the darkness of the pit, you have to boldly step forth into the light. Now is the time for confession and repentance! God eagerly awaits your return and longs to bathe you in mercy.

The steadfast love of the LORD never ceases; his mercies never come to an end; they are new every morning; great is your faithfulness. (Lamentations 3:22-23, NIV)

Do not be like the horse tied to the pole! As teacher and evangelist Oswald Chambers wrote, "Beware of paying attention or going back to what you once were, when God wants you to be something that you have never been."[2] Run in God's freedom and joy and be the person He created you to be!

Chapter 4

Guilt and Sorrow

While God overwhelmed my heart and soul with His goodness and mercy, I was also overcome with sorrow and remorse over my sin. I honestly don't know if I had ever yearned for heaven more in my life than I had during this time. The words to Charlie Hall's song, "Come For Me," would often flood my heart as I ached for Jesus. I was tired and weary. I longed for no more pain, for no more sin, and for peace...to look into the eyes of my glorious King.

I frequently poured out my heartache and sorrow to God on hundreds of journal pages the following few years after the affair. Here is a snippet of me crying out to God with regret:

Can the one that betrayed so deeply ever be used again to bring joy? Is it possible, Lord? Will I ever be anything other than the source and reminder of such incredible pain? His heart beats, yet he doesn't breathe, Lord. He sleeps at night but doesn't rest. What he thought he knew to be true turned out to be false, and what he believed to be false turned out to be true. It's not his fault, Lord—I take the blame. He would've listened had I spoken. He would've fought for me. So why did I remain silent in the chains of my prison?

I have so much regret, and my heart is so heavy. Your words reverberate in my heart. Your scripture from Isaiah 48:18, NKJV, says, "If only you had paid attention to my commands, your peace would have been like a river, your righteousness like the waves of the sea."

If only I had paid attention to your commands! Why do we make free choices that lead to bondage? Why did I not trust you? My heart is utterly broken for Garrett, but I still can't feel the depth of his pain. I wish I could.

Why?!? Why did I go down this wretched road? Never again, Lord. NEVER. God, I've inflicted wounds so deep. Bind his broken heart, Lord. Give us hope and a future. You've been so sweet and beautiful in this. You are truly amazing.

Feeling guilt, sorrow, and remorse over your sin is a godly and appropriate response, opening the gateway to running in God's freedom and joy. I would argue that if you have not felt these things, then perhaps you have not felt the total weight of your sin or begun to scratch the surface of how abhorrent sin is to God and how desperately you need Jesus. God uses guilt and sorrow over our sins to move us closer to Him and to be reconciled.

Just like many people (including myself) never intended to have a full-blown affair, David, the "man after God's own heart," also stepped onto a slippery slope and made one sinful decision after another. He is a beautiful example of working from a place of guilt and sorrow to reconciliation with the Father. Here is a quick recap from 1 Samuel chapter eleven:

- David stays home when other kings are off to war (he should be with them).

- He's up late one night and sees a beautiful woman (Bathsheba) bathing on a rooftop.

- Instead of turning his gaze away and fleeing from temptation, he lusts after her and sends messengers to find out more about her.

- He learns she is married to Uriah, a faithful soldier in David's army.

- Even after learning she is married, He *still* sends messengers to bring Bathsheba to him, and he sleeps with her.

- She becomes pregnant. So, David brings Uriah back from battle in hopes he will sleep with his wife to cover up his indiscretion.

- When Uriah refuses to sleep with his wife, David arranges to have him "killed in battle."

Wow! From all that we can tell, David never set out that sleepless night planning to have sex with another man's wife, get her pregnant, and then murder her husband because of his sinful behavior. Yet, that's precisely what happened.

Notice we don't see any remorse or guilt on David's part until the prophet, Nathan, rebukes him in chapter twelve. We know this took at least nine months because Bathsheba had already given birth to their son.

Then David said to Nathan, "I have sinned against the Lord." Nathan replied, "The Lord has taken away your sin. You are not going to die. But because by doing this you have shown utter contempt for the Lord, the son born to you will die." (2 Samuel 12:13-14, NIV)

David was finally confronted with the reality of his abhorrent sin, which would cost him (and Bathsheba) their son's life. Can you imagine the pain, the guilt, the remorse? The utter desperation before the Lord? For a week, he fasted and pleaded with the Lord to spare his son. Yet, on the seventh day, his son died.

David is a beautiful example of fully feeling guilt and sorrow over his sinful actions *and* then moving into the grace, mercy, and forgiveness of God, His King. Out of his broken spirit, he fully recognized his sin before the Lord and boldly asked for mercy and reconciliation. We can see this in David's writing in Psalm 51:

> Have mercy on me, O God, according to your unfailing love; according to your great compassion blot out my transgressions. Wash away all my iniquity and cleanse me from my sin. For I know my transgressions, and my sin is always before me. Against you, you only, have I sinned and done what is evil in your sight; so you are right in your verdict and justified when you judge.

> Surely I was sinful at birth, sinful from the time my mother conceived me. Yet you desired faithfulness even in the womb; you taught me wisdom in that secret place. Cleanse me with hyssop, and I will be clean; wash me, and I will be whiter than snow. Let me hear joy and gladness; let the bones you have crushed rejoice. Hide your face from my sins and blot out all my iniquity.

> Create in me a pure heart, O God, and renew

a steadfast spirit within me. Do not cast me from your presence or take your Holy Spirit from me. Restore to me the joy of your salvation and grant me a willing spirit, to sustain me. Then I will teach transgressors your ways, so that sinners will turn back to you.

Deliver me from the guilt of bloodshed, O God, you who are God my Savior, and my tongue will sing of your righteousness. Open my lips, Lord, and my mouth will declare your praise.

You do not delight in sacrifice, or I would bring it; you do not take pleasure in burnt offerings. My sacrifice, O God, is a broken spirit; a broken and contrite heart you, God, will not despise. (Psalm 51:1-17, NIV)

So, do you see? Feeling guilt and remorse over your sin is the pathway to confession, repentance, and reconciliation with your Savior.

And now I rejoice, not because you were
made sorrowful, but because your sorrow
led you to repentance. For you felt the sorrow that God had intended, and so were not
harmed in any way by us. (2 Corinthians
7:9-10, BSB)

Chapter 5

Confession & Repentance

Perhaps you have found yourself like me at points in your life where you have searched for others to validate a decision not to confess your sin. Or maybe you told someone about your sin but not the person who mattered the most.

Here's the deal with confession. We can often reason that we have confessed our sins because at least *someone* knows. I was guilty of this by telling one of the other men I had been physical with about my relationship with Trey. That wasn't a confession at all, even though someone else knew.

And that emotional distance I had felt from Garrett for so long? Just a few months before my confession about the affair, Garrett sat me down on that same couch in our living room and confessed to having struggled with pornography for the past eight years of our marriage.

He had told another friend about his struggle with pornography but had kept it hidden from me. It wasn't until he confessed to me, his wife, that he finally broke free. This brokenness would be another thing that we would have to navigate and mourn together.

We have an uncanny ability to confess to the people in our lives who, intentionally or not, allow that sin to remain. We must confess our sin in such a way that our lives are changed because of it.

In his writing, *My Utmost for His Highest*, Oswald Chambers stated:

> Jesus cannot come and do His work in me as long as there is anything blocking the way, whether it is something good or bad. When He comes to me, am I prepared for Him to drag every wrong thing I have ever done into the light? That is exactly where He comes. Wherever I know I am unclean is where He

will put His feet and stand, and wherever I
think I am clean is where He will remove His
feet and walk away...Get to the end of yourself where you can do nothing, but where He
does everything.[3]

**For true confession to occur, we must confess our
sin with utter brokenness and humility to the people
most impacted by our sin.** Doing so allows God to bring
what was done in the dark into the light so we may have
fellowship with him.

> If we say we have fellowship with him while
> we walk in darkness, we lie and do not prac-
> tice the truth. (1 John 1:6, ESV)

We should not blame anyone or anything else for our
actions. Instead, we must take full ownership and responsibility. I know, it's not fun. It's utterly terrifying. But, to
break free from the sin that so easily entangles, we must
confess!

Your spouse, partner, or whoever gave you their complete trust deserves to know you trampled that trust. You
have told lie after lie, and even if you somehow can gen-

uinely leave the affair behind and never cheat again, you are still living in a lie. Your spouse doesn't fully know you and is deciding to love and trust you based on partial information.

It's not only for their benefit but also yours. How can you experience the fullness of this relationship if you are not fully known and continue to live in a lie? There will always be a BUT in your mind. "But, if she only really knew me...But, if he only knew what I did...But, but, but." And, I would argue, you are much more likely to repeat your mistakes and be enslaved to sin if you don't go through the healing process of confession and repentance.

> Therefore confess your sins to each other and
> pray for each other so that you may be healed.
> The prayer of a righteous person is powerful
> and effective. (James 5:16, NIV)

We simply cannot just confess our sins. We must repent as well. Repentance goes hand-in-hand with confession. It would be incredibly difficult for a confession to be thorough, humble, and sincere without repentance.

What does repentance mean? It means "turning away; a sincere regret or remorse." Or, in pastor and theologian

John Piper's simple explanation, "Repentance means a deep change of heart that hates the sin and turns toward utter faithfulness."[4]

One of the most critical acts of repentance for me came the day after I confessed to Garrett. I quit my job effective immediately and forever slammed the door on any further contact with Trey. I turned away from him and anything associated with him and have never looked back.

The Bible is full of God's plea for us to turn away from sin and to run toward Him. God paid an unimaginable cost for our freedom from sin. Will we still sin? Absolutely! But, we can be free from the *slavery* of sin. I am no longer a slave to the sin of adultery. My husband is no longer a slave to the sin of engaging in pornography.

> What shall we say, then? Shall we go on sinning so grace may increase? By no means! We are those who have died to sin; how can we live in it any longer?...For we know that our old self was crucified with him so that the body ruled by sin might be done away with, that we should no longer be slaves to sin—because anyone who has died has been set free from sin. (Romans 6:1-2, 6-7, NIV)

Repent, then, and turn to God, so that your sins may be wiped out, that times of refreshing may come from the Lord. (Acts 3:19, NIV)

Prove by the way you live that you have repented of your sins and turned to God. (Matthew 3:8, NLT)

I needed healing, prayer, and support. And I desperately needed a change of heart. If you have hurt others in this way, you need these things, too. And whether you realize it or not, you deeply long to be fully known and fully loved. God put that desire in your heart. The only way to feel fully loved by someone on this Earth is to be fully known by them. And the only way to be in fellowship with God is to confess, to make your sin known. Then, you open the door to experience His abundant love for you.

With my confession, I felt a myriad of emotions. I felt horrified at what I had to articulate to my sweet husband of what I had done. I was terrified of what the future of our relationship may or may not be and utterly sickened by the havoc I had just unleashed upon his heart and mind.

Yet, as scandalous as it may sound, at the same time, I felt immense joy and indescribable freedom. In my heart, I knew I was finally free from this sin that entangled me and killed my spirit. Once and for all I put to death what had separated me from God and Garrett for so long. I was relieved. I had lived the last five years in the bottom of a pit with Satan's foot on my neck. Tired and weary, I felt like the walking dead.

At last, I would live in the light of God's mercy and grace. I was finally coming home into my beautiful Savior's arms. And He ran out to meet me to welcome me home, wrap me up in His embrace, and celebrate my return instead of rubbing my nose in my mistakes. No, not just mistakes—my utter defiance and rebellion. So, yes, I felt incredible joy.

It's strange to explain how I could feel joy at that moment. It even sounds sadistic in some sense that in sharing about the ultimate betrayal and horrible sin in my life that crushed Garrett's heart, I could somehow feel joy. I want to be clear—I was horrified and remorseful over what I had done and how it impacted Garrett, our marriage, our lives, and our ministry. Sorrow enveloped every part of my being. Yet, *at the same time*, God's peace and joy were ever-present. I had come home. God had missed His little girl. In His arms, I finally found where I belonged, and there just isn't any greater joy than that.

You cannot live in the freedom and joy you were created to live in without confession and repentance. You will remain like the horse tied to the pole. God desires you, all of you. He longs to pour His grace over you and to wash you white as snow. He has already paid for your sin with the death of His son, Jesus, on the cross.

You will have to live with the consequences of your sin; that is the reality whether you confess or not. Your spouse has a choice to work toward and extend forgiveness. It is their gift to give if they so choose to give it. You cannot control whether they give it, nor can you demand it. But, they need to know all of what they are choosing to forgive. And while we do not know if they will choose forgiveness, we have the assurance that God forgives us. And, if God forgives us, we can forgive ourselves!

If we confess our sins, he is faithful and just to forgive us our sins and to cleanse us from all unrighteousness. (1 John 1:9, NIV)

In his *Desiring God – Ask Pastor John* podcast, John Piper answers the question, "How Can Couples Heal After Adultery?" And I love his response, "Two miracles are required for the will of God to be done in the preservation and renewal of such a marriage. One miracle is forgiveness by the one who was wronged. And the other miracle is repentance and long-suffering—long-suffering and patience—by the one who has committed adultery."[5]

Garrett quickly committed to working toward forgiveness, but we would have a very long road ahead of us. I would also have to be patient. The day I confessed wasn't the only day I confessed. After all, I had carried on an affair for five years, and Garrett wanted to know all the details. Did I enjoy kissing him? Did we say "I love you" to one another? Did we have nicknames for each other? Did we laugh together? And so many more.

Garrett had the right to know what his wife had done, and I determined to be forthright and honest. It wasn't just up to him to have to ask all of the right questions. There were many times when I would remember something and have to go confess it to him.

At one point in time after having told Garrett so many atrocious things, Garrett summed up his pain by saying, "It's like being hit over and over again with a baseball bat. While you can really feel and identify the first few blows, after a while, it's just all pain."

Remember the spiritual attacks I experienced during the affair? The only times I encountered them again in the few years after the affair was if I had remembered something to tell Garrett but didn't tell him immediately. Satan worked hard to get his greedy hands on my heart and our marriage again.

That said, you may find yourself in a state of continual confession. Bringing all that was done in the dark out into the light may take more time than just one sitting. And it is here we find healing. No more hiding. No more lies.

Garrett and I didn't have a time limit on how long he could ask me questions. So, for about two-and-a-half years up to the point when Garrett fully forgave me, if a question came to mind related to the affair, he would ask it. And if something triggered a memory in me that I had not yet shared with him, I shared it.

I won't lie. This process was *utterly exhausting*. So, Piper nailed it on the head about having to be patient and long-suffering as the offender. It was challenging for me to go back and recount all of my horrendous sin for so long, mainly because I truly felt like I was a different person. The wife who did those things isn't who God created her to be. And when God says He removes our sin from us as far as the east is from the west, that is what I *felt* in my whole being. It was difficult trying to live fully in the freedom and grace of the Lord while having to go back and share all I had done.

Yet, Garrett had to come to a place of acceptance in his grief process. And part of that was knowing the full height and depth of the affair and working to process it. He struggled to reconcile who I am in Christ and what I had done. I believe I would never have felt fully forgiven by him had I not shared everything.

Now, for others, the offended may not want to know everything and can wholeheartedly move to a place of forgiveness. Again, your journey may be different. Some counselors may suggest you set aside specific times each day or week when you agree to discuss the affair to give both you and your spouse some room to breathe. Additionally, setting boundaries may be especially important if you have children in the house.

In walking through the aftermath of her husband's infidelity, Cindy Beall addresses this issue of asking questions in her book *Healing Your Marriage When Trust is Broken:*

> When my curiosity got the best of me and I wanted to ask Chris something, I first asked myself two questions: Why do I need to know this? And will this help me heal?

More times than not, asking the question would only hurt me more, which would not bring healing. Other times, the point of my question was just to find out when I'd been fooled, thus fueling a pride issue I was battling.

Ultimately, we must stop asking questions of our spouses because we trust our heavenly Father to make all things new again. Regardless of whether your marriage has survived, you must free yourself from the false need to gain more information because it will not help your journey to freedom. [6]

These are excellent parameters to consider in your journey. You can't dictate "the rules" for your spouse but should prayerfully consider and seek wise counsel together as to what is best for you both. Honesty and transparency are absolutely crucial, so you must be on the same page about what/when to share. Otherwise, the offended party may feel you are continuing to hide things.

And while I haven't dived into it much in this book, you may be wondering about my processing of Garrett's confession regarding his eight-year struggle with pornography.

I had my own grieving and questions to ask Garrett about what that entailed. So, in addition to my path of healing and restoration over my sin, I had to wrestle with and fully forgive Garrett for his sin.

At the time of his initial confession, I didn't feel like I had the right to grieve or be upset because I was hiding my own sin. My primary reaction was relief to finally understand the distance I had felt for so long. I was also grateful that he had begun the process of no longer being enslaved to that sin.

Unfortunately, our pastors/leaders didn't come to our aid with his confession of pornography. It was absolute crickets. NOT. ONE. WORD. I didn't realize the stark contrast it was until I saw the response to my sin a few months later. From a church standpoint, I was left absolutely alone to deal with his betrayal.

Was the response to my sin justified? Absolutely. *And* it was full of love and grace and I am forever grateful for how our church and leadership navigated these murky waters. Yet, the lack of response to Garrett's pornography confession painted a picture of how easy it is as a church to dismiss the hurt and betrayal of a spouse affected by their partner's sin with pornography. It felt as if it is so normalized as a struggle that it doesn't warrant tender care and empathy.

To this day, I come across people that completely ignore this part of the brokenness in our marriage, and/or quickly accuse me of trying to justify my affair when I openly talk about Garrett's struggle with pornography and the hurt that it caused. That breaks my heart, and I am sorry if you have had a similar experience. I share my experience in this realm simply because I want you to know your hurt matters and needs to be grieved!

And in only God's perfect way, He allowed some sense of understanding on both of our parts to the hurt child within who acted out in these sinful ways. I could understand that Garrett engaging with pornography wasn't about the women on the computer screen, but about anxiety and brokenness within him. And on some level, he could understand my affair wasn't about sex. It was about trying to fill a more profound void within.

Garrett and I worked together to be free. We grieved and became angry. We both suffered greatly over our own sins and the hurt we caused one another. Yet, we chose minute by minute to fight for one another together with Jesus, and He is oh so faithful.

Chapter 6

Will God Forgive Me?

When I remained incredibly entrenched in my sin, I believed so many lies from the enemy. One of these lies was God will not forgive me because I had sinned far too great and for too long. He will never take me back. I just needed to accept who I was—a hopeless, helpless adulteress.

The day after my confession, Garrett met with a fellow church staff member and friend to tell him about the affair. It was a sickening feeling to sit at home knowing Garrett was articulating my horrendous sin to others. Later in the week, all of the church leaders would gather to learn about my infidelity. #funtimes

After what felt like hours, Garrett finally came home with a dozen pink roses in hand. I cried as I embraced him, thinking, *how can such beauty be extended to such a wretched being?* He was already working so hard to extend love to me with his shattered heart.

Garrett then mentioned a storm was rolling in as he drove home. It reminded us of our summer at Myrtle Beach when we first met and God brought us together. We would go down to the beach to watch the lightning and listen to the thunder as the rain gently fell on our faces; we felt God's awesomeness in those times.

We opened the blinds in our living room and sat on the floor in the dark, holding hands in silence, with so much pain and uncertainty flooding our hearts. As we watched the rain pound against the windows, I felt like God reminded me of the lyrics to the song by Todd Agnew, "Grace Like Rain." I could almost feel God's grace pouring over me like rain washing my stains away. The song's words rang true in my soul and echoed in my heart.

God then brought our wedding song to mind, "A Page is Turned," by Bebo Norman. The lyrics speak of a little boy growing up and how God is preparing for him the one he is to marry, and a little girl growing up and how God is preparing for her the one she is to marry. And, all the while, God is all over their lives, picking them up when they come undone, giving them a second chance, and washing them in the rain of His grace. This song has spoken a lot to us over the years and it shouted to me in this moment.

As the words to these songs reverberated in the chambers of my broken heart, the rain came down harder and faster. There was a clear, visible, and noticeable difference...the rain pounded so hard against the glass I seriously thought it would break.

I felt God speaking directly into my heart and soul, expressing His overwhelming grace and love for me, shouting to my heart that every single, dirty part of me and what I had done was fully washed away by His grace. I was spotless and made new. And God's grace does not run out—He will always give me a second chance. Even if it is the 100,000th time I have messed up, God is there to give me another chance.

Lastly, I felt God assuring me that He would see us through this tumultuous storm in our lives. He would hold us up as we were so undone, and we would dance once again. I clung to the hope God shared, and I gladly bathed in the rain of His grace.

ell

His grace is the same for you. I am not the exception. His mercies are new every day, and He truly casts our sin from us as far as the east is from the west!

We must kick Satan and his lies to the curb and cling to God's truth about who He really is. The enemy wants nothing more than to leave us in a state of hopelessness and despair. He wants us to put off hope as long as we live. Why? Because, "Hope deferred makes the heart sick, but a longing fulfilled is a tree of life." (Proverbs 13:12, NIV)

To defer simply means to put off, to postpone. Don't defer the hope you have in Jesus! God will forgive adultery! Jesus Christ has already paid the penalty for your sin. Your affair was included when God the Father poured out His wrath on His perfect son, Jesus. Jesus paid the death penalty for your affair, all of your sins, once and for all on the cross. **To question whether or not He will forgive us is to question the purpose and power of Jesus' death on the cross and resurrection. It is FINISHED!**

But our High Priest offered himself to God
as a single sacrifice for sins, good for all time.

Then he sat down in the place of honor at God's right hand. (Hebrews 10:12, NLT)

Let's consider these additional truths:

God removes our sins from us. "...as far as the east is from the west, so far has he removed our transgressions from us." (Psalm 103:12, NIV)

God completely cleans us. "Come now, let us reason together, says the Lord: though your sins are like scarlet, they shall be as white as snow; though they are red like crimson, they shall become like wool." (Isaiah 1:18, ESV)

Like the prodigal son's father in Luke chapter 15, **God runs out to meet us when we decide to come home.** There is no lecture, no rubbing our noses in our mistakes. Instead, God throws a robe upon our shoulders, a ring upon our finger, and declares, "Let's celebrate! My precious child has returned home!"

God does not treat us as our sins deserve.
"...he does not treat us as our sins deserve or repay us according to our iniquities." (Psalm 103:10, NIV)

God remembers our sins no more. "For I will forgive their wickedness and will remember their sins no more." (Jeremiah 31:34, NIV)

God is merciful. "The Lord is gracious and full of compassion, Slow to anger and great in mercy. The Lord is good to all, And His tender mercies are over all His works." (Psalm 145:8-9, NKJV)

God is full of grace. "For it is by grace you have been saved, through faith—and this is not from yourselves, it is the gift of God—not by works, so that no one can boast." (Ephesians 2:8-9, NIV)

So, friend, if you are struggling to believe God will forgive you, I am here, as living proof, to shout from the mountaintop that He WILL. He already HAS. And God doesn't just stop at forgiveness. He cleanses us from all unrighteousness, calls us sons and daughters, and is giddy when we come home.

Whether you have or have not placed your faith in Jesus, He has already paid the price to reconcile you to Himself, and all He longs for is for you to come as you are—to repent, hate your sin, and turn away from it. To run home to your Abba, Father. He will run out to meet you, lift your head, scoop you into His arms, and dance with delight over you.

And if our all-powerful, mighty, and holy God forgives you, can you forgive yourself?

Chapter 7

Can I Forgive Myself?

A friend of mine once told me about how she came home one day to find their "discipline stick" missing from its usual place. As she walked down the hall, she found her ten-year-old son holding that stick, spanking himself for something for which he felt he deserved punishment.

And God gave me a picture of us as His children grabbing that stick and spanking ourselves. We hold that stick and determine our own punishment for our wrongdoing. Can you envision a child doing that? Yet, we do this all the time.

When we perpetually beat ourselves up over our sin, we essentially declare that what God did by pouring out the punishment we rightfully deserve onto His perfect and only Son is not enough. We reject God's gift and take matters into our own hands because somehow, we know better than God. No matter how much punishment we lay on ourselves, it will never be enough. It can never pay for our sin. We remain stuck and give Satan the victory by not taking God at His word.

Should we feel guilt and remorse over our sin? Yes, 100%. We covered that earlier on. However, our sin has been atoned for and our guilt removed. I love this section in Isaiah when he is commissioned as a prophet and witnesses the holy presence of the Lord:

> "Woe to me!" I cried. "I am ruined!" For I am a man of unclean lips, and I live among a people of unclean lips, and my eyes have seen the King, the Lord Almighty.

> Then one of the seraphs flew to me with a live coal in his hand, which he had taken with tongs from the altar. With it he touched my mouth and said, "See, this has touched your

lips; your guilt is taken away and your sin atoned for." (Isaiah 6:5-7, NIV)

Your guilt is taken away and your sin atoned for! So often, we continue to punish ourselves as if it is the "holy" thing to do. We still must live with the earthly consequences of our sins, but we do not have to continuously live in guilt and shame.

As a parent of two beautiful children, it would break my heart to see them continue to punish themselves, living in guilt and shame knowing they have been forgiven. To remain in that place of self-loathing keeps us from living in the fullness of life that Christ has freely given us with His death on the cross. It keeps us from the good works He has set in advance for us to do.

As our perfect Father in heaven, how much more must it break His heart when we, His children, attempt to take back the guilt of the sin that He paid so much to remove from us? He has already paid the ultimate punishment so why do we continue to punish ourselves? We must put down the stick!

I believe we have not yet fully accepted God's forgiveness if we have not forgiven ourselves for our wrongdoing.

Once I accepted God's forgiveness, here are the questions I wrestled with:

If the God of the Universe, the Holy and Perfect One, freely forgives me and covers me with His grace, who am I to not extend forgiveness and grace to myself? Am I above God? Are my standards and idea of perfection greater than God's?

Author C.S. Lewis addresses this idea beautifully, "I think that if God forgives us we must forgive ourselves. Otherwise, it's almost like setting up ourselves as a higher tribunal than Him."[7]

Forgiving yourself does not excuse or justify your sinful behavior. Instead, it allows you to live in the truth of who He declares you are: holy, blameless, and dearly loved. It enables you to break free from Satan's foothold and step into a life of freedom and joy.

In her wealth of experience, therapist and writer Beverly Engel states, "I believe that self-forgiveness is the most powerful step you can take to rid yourself of debilitating shame... Self-forgiveness is not only recommended but absolutely essential if we wish to become emotionally healthy and have peace of mind...If you do not forgive yourself, the shame you carry will compel you to continue to act in harmful ways toward others and yourself. And forgiving yourself will help you to heal another layer of shame and free you to continue becoming a better human being. Without the burden of self-hatred you have been carrying around you can literally transform your life."[8]

I know it can feel scandalous to have the audacity to forgive yourself and live in freedom and joy after committing such a horrendous sin. But, God's love is *outrageous*. His sacrifice for your forgiveness and freedom is nothing but scandalous.

It may be hard for those around you to see you step into this grace and forgiveness. I experienced this. Friends from our church who believe in and preach God's forgiveness and goodness still wanted, in their humanness, to see punishment of some kind. It was challenging for them to see Garrett doing the work to forgive me and be reconciled to me. Didn't I just deserve to be left in the dust? Didn't I deserve punishment?

The answer is yes; that is 100% what my sin deserved. BUT GOD. This truth bears repeating—God does not treat us as our sin deserves.

> ...he does not treat us as our sins deserve or repay us according to our iniquities. For as high as the heavens are above the earth, so

great is his love for those who fear him; as far as the east is from the west, so far has he removed our transgressions from us. As a father has compassion on his children, so the Lord has compassion on those who fear him; for he knows how we are formed, he remembers that we are dust. (Psalm 103:10-14, NIV)

Keep your eyes on your perfect Father in heaven and not on those around you struggling with condemnation. Their condemnation is their issue to take to God.

Now, I don't mean others can't feel hurt or betrayed by your actions. The consequences of sin reach far and wide and there may be many relationships that need healing and reconciliation. But for those that simply desire punishment and want to cast stones—that is for the Lord to deal with their hearts. Hold onto the truth of Romans 8:1, NIV, "Therefore, there is now no condemnation for those who are in Christ Jesus."

After having sinned so greatly, I now have a much deeper understanding and gratefulness for God's grace and mercy than I ever had before my egregious failure. Consider this interaction Jesus had with Simon:

Jesus answered him, "Simon, I have something to tell you."

"Tell me, teacher," he said.

"Two people owed money to a certain moneylender. One owed him five hundred denarii, and the other fifty. Neither of them had the money to pay him back, so he forgave the debts of both. Now which of them will love him more?"

Simon replied, "I suppose the one who had the bigger debt forgiven."

"You have judged correctly," Jesus said.

Then he turned toward the woman and said to Simon, "Do you see this woman? I came into your house. You did not give me any water for my feet, but she wet my feet with her tears and wiped them with her hair. You did not give me a kiss, but this woman, from the time I entered, has not stopped kissing my feet. You did not put oil on my head, but she has poured perfume on my feet. Therefore, I tell you, her many sins have been forgiven—as her great love has shown. But whoever has been forgiven little loves little." (Luke 7:41-47, NIV)

So often I felt like this woman, weeping tears of gratitude onto Jesus' feet and washing them with my hair. My debt is great, and I have been forgiven. I was and am so incredibly thankful and humbled at His love for me. Sometimes I wonder what my life would look like now had I not grasped a hold of God's sweet forgiveness and grace for me.

Similarly, I wonder what if the Apostle Paul hadn't fully accepted God's forgiveness? I can only imagine there were people around him casting judgment and wanting punishment for all he had done. After all, Paul had made a living hating and killing followers of Jesus. What if he had listened to all the naysayers?

In his letter to Timothy, Paul said this about himself, "Here is a trustworthy saying that deserves full acceptance: Christ Jesus came into the world to save sinners—of whom I am the worst." (1 Timothy 1:15, NIV)

Paul's life and writings exemplify this deep understanding and thankfulness for God's grace and mercy. He and the world would have missed out on God's extraordinary plan for his life if he had not stepped fully into God's forgiveness, thereby forgiving himself.

And what about Peter? Look at the impact he had on the kingdom during his time and still today. He had declared to Jesus, "Even if all fall away on account of you, I never will." (Matthew 26:33, NIV)

Yet, he did the very thing he never thought he would do. He hated that he had denied his friend, his Savior, three times. When he realized what he had done, "...he went outside and wept bitterly." (Matthew 26:75, NIV)

Peter felt guilt and remorse over his actions. What if he deemed himself unfit for the calling Jesus gave him to feed and take care of His sheep? What if he just stayed in a state of self-loathing and punishment?

And I even wonder about Judas. According to Matthew 27:3-4, NIV, "When Judas, who had betrayed him, saw that Jesus was condemned, he was seized with remorse and returned the thirty silver coins to the chief priests and elders. 'I have sinned,' he said. 'For I have betrayed innocent blood.' 'What is that to us?' they replied. 'That is your responsibility.' So Judas threw the money into the temple and left. Then he went away and hanged himself."

The story of Judas is sad, although I see myself in him. He has forever been branded as "he who betrayed Jesus." That's big time. And like him, I could forever have been branded "she who cheated on and betrayed her husband, the adulteress." What if Judas hadn't killed himself and instead encountered Jesus after the resurrection, like the other disciples?

I wholeheartedly believe Jesus would have extended him grace and forgiveness. I think He would have spoken to Judas' identity not as the betrayer but as a dearly loved child of God. What would Judas' impact on the kingdom have been had he stuck around for this encounter?

Friend, your identity is not defined by your sins. God defines your identity. What matters most is who God says you are. Because of having Jesus in your heart, God looks upon you as holy and dearly loved, without spot or blemish. You are His workmanship! He exclaims His love for you and His delight in you! What will you and the world miss out on if *you* don't forgive yourself?

The Bible is full of story after story of people who blew it big time. You are not alone. Yet, God picked them up, gave them a second chance, and set their feet on the right path. He longs to do the same with you!

Chapter 8

What are These Wounds, Lord?

Less than a week after I confessed my affair to Garrett, I was in Italy with my mom. We had planned this trip long beforehand, and both Garrett and our pastor thought it was best I still go. So, with much trepidation and uncertainty, I went. I had not yet told my mom of the affair nor my confession to Garrett—that would come once we settled into our hotel room in Rome. #morefuntimes

I was eager to get some time with the Lord on my long and uncomfortable flight to Rome. I read a quote by author John Eldredge earlier in the week that made me curious. "A wound that goes unacknowledged and unwept is a wound that cannot heal. A wound you've embraced is a wound that cannot heal. A wound you think you deserved is a wound that cannot heal."[9] So, I asked the Lord, "What are my wounds?"

While there was absolutely no excuse or blaming my past in any way for my affair, I wanted to better understand why I did the things I did and suspected there were areas of healing needed surrounding my parents' divorce. I was now thirty-three years old, and growing up, we just moved on after the divorce. We survived. And after all, I dearly love my stepmom, my half-sisters, and my entire family. Everything turned out okay, so what was the big deal?

Eager to dive in, I read through the first chapter of *The Adult Child of Divorce* by Bob Burns and Michael J. Brisset, Jr., and flipped to the workbook section. Perhaps some nugget of insight, some revelation, would help me begin to understand my egregious behavior. It asked question after question surrounding details of the divorce, to which the only answer I had to nearly all of the questions was "I don't remember, I don't remember."

In frustration, I set the book aside and opened my journal. Blaise Pascal, a French mathematician, philosopher, and Catholic theologian wrote, "We know ourselves so little."[10] I knew myself so little, and I was ready to sit quietly before the Lord. I asked God to help me remember, to learn about myself, and to get a picture of my past hurt. Instantly, I began writing memory after random memory, page after page.

They bombarded my mind. I remembered rushing home following a gymnastics meet the morning my mom left. I wanted to show off my third-place trophy to my mom, only to find she was gone. My grandmother told me I was a burden to my mom. After barely turning thirteen, an older neighborhood boy said he wanted to date me but not unless I had sex with him. I wrote pages of comments as a young teenager about my body, but so few about me as a whole person. Twenty pages later, with a very cramped hand and tears pouring down my face, I began to picture a hurt little girl.

God was ushering me into a season of incredible intimacy and healing with Him. During this season, He showed me so much about who I am in Him and who He truly is. He gently took me by the hand to teach me. And one of His sweet lessons came during that same hike in Estes Park, Colorado, a few months after my confession.

Based on the recommendations of a few friends, I eagerly set off for a hike to nearby Moraine Park. As I embarked on my little adventure, I prayed, "God, I am here. I am listening. I just want to hear what you want to say to me today." So I set off in silence, hoping to hear something from the Lord.

I followed the squiggly line on my relatively worthless map and came across my first bend in the trail. As I took a few steps around the bend, I heard a rustling in the tall grass to my right. *Oh, no. What if there's a snake in there? And what if it bites me? And what if it is poisonous?*

And God seemed to ask, "So, what if it is poisonous?"

"Well, we'd have to get the poison out; otherwise, it would kill me," I replied.

And God began to teach me. "Exactly. Brenna, you have been bitten by a snake. The most dangerous snake of all—a deceitful snake that hisses untruths and lies. He is poisonous. And, if we don't get that poison out of your system, it will cause death. Death of your heart. Of life. Of freedom. Of joy."

Yet, for so long, I had been entirely unaware it was poison inside of me that I needed to deal with. I had to acknowledge past hurts and grieve them. I had to identify the lies I believed and understand how those affected my view of God and myself. I had to combat the lies I was fed because of my great sin with the affair. This poison inside was killing me, and I didn't even know it! It robbed me of life, freedom, and joy. And, now, I had to get it out.

With the help of my dear counselor, Kelly, and a lot of time with the Lord, I began to identify my past wounds and how my experiences affected my core beliefs—the deep, unconscious beliefs I held inside my heart about who I was and who God is. With the understanding of how my experiences helped shape my core beliefs, I could better understand my behavior because it's all connected. Our core beliefs impact our thoughts, which affect our feelings which all ultimately impact and determine our behavior.

A couple of significant experiences I had as a child shaped my core beliefs. First and foremost, when I was eight years old, my dad had an affair and got the "other woman" pregnant. For the record, the "other woman", whom I love dearly, has been my stepmother since I was nine years old. I am so thankful she is part of my life. That pregnancy resulted in my first half-sister. Another pregnancy shortly after that gave me another half-sister. My whole family loves the Lord and God has truly redeemed what started out so broken. I have a wonderful family and can't imagine my life without them.

However, I came to recognize at thirty-three years old that I could be thankful for and love my family *and* still process the hurt that came about because of my dad's affair. Affairs and divorce cause trauma and that trauma needs to be grieved.

I had been the apple of my daddy's eye. At eight years old, before the divorce, I did not doubt he loved me. He danced with me and delighted in me. We had a secure connection. However, when he had an affair, my parents separated. My mom moved to Washington state (we lived in Michigan at the time), and my younger brother and I stayed behind to finish the school year with my dad.

My little girl heart didn't understand the separation despite my parents explaining what was happening to the best of their ability. I simply couldn't fully comprehend the brokenness of the situation. Just all of a sudden, my mom was gone.

When the summer rolled around a couple of months later, my brother and I moved states away to live with my mom. Shortly after that, my dad chose to stay with his new family, and my parents officially divorced.

What indirect messages did my little girl's heart receive from my dad in particular? Now, keep in mind, my dad still loved me. I do not doubt that. He never, ever verbally said these words to me, nor do I believe he ever thought them. I know he loved me deeply then as he does now. Yet, his *actions spoke deep into the core of my being.* I didn't realize it at the time, but here are the messages my heart received:

I am not worth it.
I am not enough.
I am not wanted.
I am not valuable.
I am not seen.
I am not worth knowing.
Another little girl is more important than me.

As a young girl, I had a recurring dream for years after my parents' divorce. In the dream, my dad, my brother, and I were on a small, curved stone bridge. My dad fished over the side of the bridge and was preoccupied. My brother played on the bridge and fell off, dangling from the side.

I would desperately try to get my dad's attention to help save my brother, but he wouldn't acknowledge me or my brother. He just kept fishing. And even though my dad fished in this dream, the water under the bridge turned to pavement as my brother was about to fall. The dream would end in various ways with me always trying to find some way to save my brother. Suddenly I would ride a bike down to catch him, or I would run down to save him.

Our body has a way of exhibiting and processing trauma even if we aren't aware of it or are cognitively dealing with it. Trauma makes an imprint on us. I believe this recurring dream was one of the ways my body tried to process hurt due to my parents' divorce.

Bessel A. van der Kolk explains the impact of trauma in his book, *The Body Keeps the Score*:

> We have learned that trauma is not just an event that took place sometime in the past; it is also the imprint left by that experience on mind, brain, and body. This imprint has ongoing consequences for how the human organism manages to survive in the present. Trauma results in a fundamental reorganization of the way mind and brain manage perceptions. It changes not only how we think and what we think about, but also our very capacity to think.[11]

Experiencing a divorce is trauma. And while the seed of shame had been planted due to my dad's actions, it was later watered by my mom.

She was just doing the best she could. It's not like life turned out the way she dreamed of either. For several years after the divorce, my brother and I lived with my single, full-time working mother. At first, we lived with her at her parents' small house in Federal Way, Washington. Then we eventually moved into various apartments—a far cry from what we had when our family was together in Michigan.

In seventh grade, I started rebelling. I constantly butted heads with my mom, which also affected my brother. I would skip school and steal things. It seemed like I was out of control. Then, one day, I made the ultra-wise decision to blast Eazy-E out of our apartment window when my mom was gone.

If you are unfamiliar with Eazy-E, this is the "gangsta rap" era of my life and the lyrics are *not* family-friendly. My mom received a call from the apartment manager complaining about my behavior.

With everything spinning out of control, my mom sought counsel from her pastor at the time regarding what to do with me. He suggested she kick me out and have me go live with her parents. I didn't learn about the pastor's advice until recently as I prepared to write this book; I just knew my mom kicked me out and that is the wound my heart carried for all these years. My mom deeply regrets taking that advice, and I am shocked it was the advice she received. Yet, desperate times called for desperate measures. Again, she didn't know what to do to help the situation, but my young heart didn't understand that at the time.

As a result, on top of the messages I received from my dad because of his affair and our family subsequently splitting up, I received similar indirect messages from my mom:

I am not worth fighting for.
I am too much.
I am not wanted.
I am not valuable.

Again, she never said any of these things directly to me. She loved me and honestly tried to figure out what was best for everyone, given the situation. Yet, my heart was significantly impacted.

During that time, my brother and I stayed at Grandma and Grandpa's house every day after school until my mom got off work and took us home. Except, now, when she arrived after work, only my brother would get to go home with her. I was left behind.

I can't even begin to describe my loneliness and sadness. I didn't have a great relationship with my grandparents. I pretty much lived in the back bedroom as I didn't feel comfortable or welcome in the rest of the house.

If the indirect messages weren't enough, my grandmother was much more direct. One day after school, I had done something to tick her off. She grabbed a wooden spoon and started spanking my nearly thirteen-year-old butt. It broke (the spoon, not my butt).

In response to the spoon breaking, I quipped some snarky response that sent her over the edge. She grabbed a flyswatter and started chasing me back to my bedroom, hitting me with it over and over again.

The flyswatter didn't hurt. Instead, as she hit me, she shouted, "You are such a burden to your mom! You are such a burden!" These words cut to my core.

My younger brother stood in the doorway to my bedroom, yelling and pleading with my grandmother to stop. I still remember the terrified look on his face. Honestly, I don't remember how it stopped or how long it continued. But she did *not* quit right away. It wasn't until I sat with my counselor after the affair and recounted the story that we began to scratch the surface of how deeply this experience wounded me.

Maybe something inside of you feels like you are a burden to those around you. Perhaps someone has verbally told you those words. I'm so sorry if that's the case. I can tell you, in my situation, it was both. And, deep down in my heart, it solidified a core belief that I was a burden.

So how did my core beliefs affect my behavior? In the recesses of my heart, I ultimately believed I was unwanted, undesirable, and not valuable. Yet, I was unaware of these feelings on the surface. In my brokenness, I turned to ways to feel wanted and desirable. Make sense?

Again, I do not blame my past for my actions. I take 100% responsibility for the sinful choices that I made. *Yet*, by seeking this kind of understanding I acknowledge the areas of my life that need healing so that I don't go down that road ever again.

Unfortunately, I failed to recognize my pattern before I got married. While dating in college, if there was some length of time where I was physically distant from my current boyfriend, I wound up engaging in a brief physical encounter with an ex-boyfriend. Something in my heart and mind couldn't handle the distance. But, I never thought in a million years I would do something like that once I got married. Yet, I did. Only this time, it wasn't physical distance. It was a spiritual distance from the Lord and an emotional distance from my husband.

ele

Beyond how our experiences affect our beliefs and interactions with people, they also impact our heartfelt view of God.

While we can read our Bible, listen to sermons, and even believe in our heads who God says He is, our experiences often subconsciously affect what our *heart actually believes* about God.

In his book *Healing of Memories,* David A. Seamands states,

> The most determinative factor is our "feltness" of who God is and what He is really like. It is surprising the number of genuine Christians who are caught in an inner conflict between what they think about God and what they feel about God (and how He feels toward them)...Years of experience have taught me that regardless of how much correct doctrine Christians may know, until

they have a picture and a sense that God is truly good and gracious, there can be no lasting spiritual victory in their lives.[12]

While my head believed all the things about God I learned in Sunday school, I had to know what my heart actually felt. For instance, if I am alone in a room with God, where am I in relation to Him? What is the look on His face? How do I feel about being there? And in thinking through these things, I realized I was at the opposite end of the room from God. In my heart, He was the God that did not see me and the God that didn't care. He didn't even realize I was there.

I projected my experiences in life onto whom I believed God was in my heart. The hurt little girl inside me rebelled, crying out for attention. "Do you see me now, God? Do you even care?" I had to come face-to-face with the reality that I had been letting my feelings influence my "truth" about God. But, as missionary and author Amy Carmichael eloquently wrote:

Our feelings do not affect God's facts. They may blow up, like clouds, and cover the eternal things that we do most truly believe.

We may not see the shining of the promises—but they still shine! His strength is not for one moment less because of our human weakness.[13]

Through this sacred journey of reflection and healing, my heartfelt view of God began to shift. No longer is He the God that doesn't see me, nor the God that doesn't care. Now, when I am in a room alone with Him, He not only sees me, but He draws me close. I am sitting upon His lap with my head resting on His chest. He tenderly catches the tears streaming down my cheeks and preserves every one of them in His bottle. I can look Him in His eyes and see His delight in me, His precious little girl. I can feel Him pick me up and twirl me around with singing and dancing.

I am forever grateful to know Him the way I do now. My prayer is that you would know God in this way, too!

Chapter 9

Get the Poison Out

On top of the indirect messages I received from both of my parents, the episode with my grandmother solidified in my heart for so many years that I wasn't just a burden to my mom, but I was also a burden to this world.

I had finally come to understand why I was so easily triggered and defensive when corrected, or when it was pointed out I did something "wrong." And, by "wrong," I mean even the smallest things, like when my husband would comment about how I pulled into the garage or how I loaded the dishwasher.

It would shake me. Why? It wasn't that I just *did* something wrong or unsatisfactorily, but deeply rooted in my heart was the belief that *I WAS WRONG*. All of me was not right or good. **This feeling is the essence of a shame-based identity.**

So, what is shame? Here is what Tim Sledge says about shame in his book, *Making Peace with Your Past*:

> Shame is a deep-seated feeling that something is fundamentally wrong with me. Guilt is about what I have done. Shame is about who I am.

> Having no opportunity to process a painful event can lock the emotions of the trauma in place for decades and can contribute to a shame-based identity. Whether the shame and guilt are communicated directly or indirectly, they translate into a shame-based identity and a guilt-laden thought process in the child.

> This type of shame does not reside in one small corner of a person's identity. It infiltrates all feelings and thoughts...shame always lingers beneath the surface of conscious thoughts. Even though shame permeates the

individual's identity, he or she may not recognize its presence...Ultimately, it will make
the person feel ashamed for existing.[14]

If you are struggling with feeling like a burden or that
you just aren't suitable for this world, maybe that feeling
stems from something much more profound—SHAME.
And it is so essential to understand shame's place in our
lives. As Curt Thompson, MD, says in his book *The Soul
of Shame,* "to know your story is to know shame's place in
it." He further explains what is necessary to begin healing
from shame:

> ...we see how shame's healing encompasses
> the counterintuitive act of turning toward
> what we are most terrified of...it is in the
> *movement toward another*, toward connec-
> tion with someone who is safe, that we come
> to know life and freedom from this prison.[15]

In the past, I had turned away from my shame and
other people. Instead, metaphorically speaking, I simply
put Band-Aids over snake bites. Yet all the while, the poison, and these deeply rooted beliefs remained and festered

within me. Beverly Engel, a therapist who writes for *Psychology Today*, summarizes the myriad of problems that shame is responsible for:

- self-criticism and self-blame;

- self-neglect;

- self-destructive behaviors;

- self-sabotaging behavior;

- perfectionism;

- the belief that you do not deserve good things;

- intense rage;

- acting out against society;

- continuing to repeat the cycle of abuse through either victim behavior or abusive behaviors.[16]

Can you relate to any of these? We must get the poison out! And a critical step to get the poison out is to identify these wounds, grieve them, and replace lies with God's truth.

Until we allow God to heal our deepest hurts, we cannot experience the fullness of the joy and freedom He has created us to live in. We will repeatedly fail to change our behavior because our core beliefs about God and ourselves are not in line with God's truth.

My biggest go-to Band-Aid was seeking love and affirmation from others. Surely love and affirmation from others would combat the hurt I experienced and the lies I believed, right? If others accept me and say I am loved, then the messages I received when I was younger, that I was a burden and unwanted, couldn't possibly be true! Yet, it was just a bandage over a snake bite. No real healing or change occurred.

My secondary cover-up was defensiveness, through good-ole finger-pointing. "There's not anything wrong with me; it's you!" I believe my defensiveness was born out of protection from my shame-based identity. I *still* struggle with defensiveness.

Have you been putting Band-Aids over snake bites instead of getting the poison out of your system? What are the ways you attempt to cover up your wounds? Some examples might be:

- Pornography

- Gambling

- Alcohol

- Drugs/numbing

- Self-harm

- Sexually addictive behavior

- Busyness

- Perfectionism

- Achievement/success

- Avoidance

- Relational codependency

- Shopping

Now, here's the real kicker. Oftentimes, we put bandages on top of other bandages. So, for example, if pornography is your initial way to cover up a wound or a false belief, you put another Band-Aid on top of it by simply trying to *control your behavior* in your own strength.

Maybe you're successful for a while and abstain. You set boundaries with your computer. Maybe, you tell a trusted friend of your struggle. You do everything you can in your strength to restrict yourself.

Don't get me wrong. Having healthy boundaries and accountability in your life is a wise and good thing. Yet, more often than not, they won't allow you to experience true freedom because they only address your behavior. It winds up just being another Band-Aid. There is something much deeper that must also be dealt with.

So, what are your wounds?

Perhaps you can matter-of-factly tell others your life story without much emotion or thought as to how your life experiences must have felt. That was me. "My dad had an affair, and my parents divorced when I was eight. My brother and I went to live with my mom in Washington state, and my dad remarried. Now, I have a stepmom and two half-sisters, and our family is great!" The end.

Or, perhaps you have been wounded so deeply you can't even recall your experiences. While your mind protected you from your traumatic past, your heart still received messages that significantly impacted your core beliefs about yourself and the world around you. If this is you, I highly recommend working with a Christian trauma counselor who can come alongside you with God to start unpacking your pain.

Ask God for help; He will tenderly guide you and hold you up. He is with you! Seek help from safe people as you navigate these feelings and identify wounds from your past. God can use other people to help you on this journey. I don't know what I would have done without the tender care and guidance I received to help me unpack and grieve my past.

Chapter 10

Who Do You Think You Are?

"**S**lut!" There was no mistaking what I had just been called. But it wasn't Garrett who called me a slut. And I didn't call myself a slut. So, who was it?

About three months after I confessed my affair to Garrett, we had a tough day with one another. I could feel the anger of all the hurt and betrayal build up inside of him as we argued.

We took a little bit of time apart, sitting in our hurt for a while. Eventually, we worked to reconnect with one another which led us to be physically intimate. Physical intimacy was an area that God quickly redeemed after my confession, as it had been broken for so long. I understand this may not be the case for everyone. We each will have our own journey in this realm.

Yet, as we began to make love, I heard the accusation clearly. "Slut!" Again, Garrett didn't say it. Even with all the extreme brokenness of his heart, he had never called me anything like that. It was clear that Satan, the accuser, was calling me names.

Garrett could tell something was going on in my heart and I was upset. We stopped making love, and he just held me. I cried and told him what happened. He apologized that I was called that name and prayed for me. He whispered in my ear, "Angel. That's the word I want you to hear—Angel."

Now, here's the thing about Satan. *Everything* that comes out of his mouth is a lie. Oftentimes, he twists and manipulates the truth to accomplish his evil, but there is absolutely no truth in him. He will do everything in his power to convince you that your identity is anything other than a forgiven, loved, and cherished child of the King.

I've said it before, and I will say it again. Your sin or mistakes do not define your identity. Likewise, the sin done to you does not define your identity. Your identity is defined by God. *Period.*

One of the biggest lies I believed for so long while being enslaved to the sin of my affair was, "This is just who I am." My identity became "adulteress." Hmmm. I wonder where that thought came from.

> ...He was a murderer from the beginning, not holding to the truth, for there is no truth in him. When he lies, he speaks his native language, for he is a liar and the father of lies. (John 8:44, NIV)

In Matthew chapter four, we even see Satan trying to manipulate Jesus himself in the desert by quoting scripture. He manipulated God's own Word in an effort to tempt Jesus. Wow. That's gutsy.

Then the devil took him to the holy city and had him stand on the highest point of the temple. "If you are the Son of God," he said, "throw yourself down. For it is written:

> 'He will command his angels concerning you, and they will lift you up in their hands, so that you will not strike your foot against a stone.'" Jesus answered him, "It is also writ-

ten: 'Do not put the Lord your God to the test." (Matthew 4:5-7, NIV)

Now, I am not "special" in any way. Just as Satan tempts and accuses me, I know he works tirelessly to tempt and accuse you.

So, what are we to do when the accusations come? We must take our thoughts captive and hold them up to God's truth.

We see this instruction in 2 Corinthians 10:5, NIV, "We demolish arguments and every pretension that sets itself up against the knowledge of God, and we take captive every thought to make it obedient to Christ."

We have to ask whether the thought or accusation is congruent with God's Word. God's Word is full of truth about who we are in Christ, who God is, and how we have victory in Jesus. We must renew our minds!

> Do not conform to the pattern of this world, but be transformed by the renewing of your mind. Then you will be able to test and approve what God's will is—his good, pleasing and perfect will. (Romans 12:2, NIV)

So, in looking at my example of being called a "slut," I can turn to God's Word and see what *He* says about me. If I have accepted Jesus as my Lord and Savior, who died once and for all to atone all of my sins, God calls me many things, but *never* a slut. So, here is the truth about who God says I am:

He says I am forgiven. "If we confess our sins, he is faithful and just and will forgive us our sins and purify us from all unrighteousness." (1 John 1:9, NIV)

He says I am clean, and my sins are washed away. "Our sins are washed away and we are made clean because Christ gave His own body as a gift to God. He did this once for all time." (Hebrews 10:10, NLV)

He says my sins have been removed from me. "As far as the east is from the west, so far does he remove our transgressions from us." (Psalm 103:12, NIV)

He says I am delighted in (NOT because of what I do or do not do, but simply because I am God's child!). "For the LORD your God is living among you. He is a mighty Savior. He will take delight in you with gladness.

With his love, he will calm all your fears. He will rejoice over you with joyful songs." (Zephaniah 3:17, NLT)

He says I am holy and blameless in His sight. "Yet now he has reconciled you to himself through the death of Christ in his physical body. As a result, he has brought you into his own presence, and you are holy and blameless as you stand before him without a single fault." (Colossians 1:22, NLT)

He says I am redeemed. "But now thus says the Lord, he who created you, O Jacob, he who formed you, O Israel: 'Fear not, for I have redeemed you; I have called you by name, you are mine.'" (Isaiah 43:1 ESV)

He says I am His child. "But as many as received Him, to them He gave the right to become children of God, even to those who believe in His name..." (John 1:12, NKJV)

Finally, He says I am loved and that absolutely *nothing* can separate me from the love of God. "Who shall separate us from the love of Christ? Shall trouble or hardship or persecution or famine or nakedness or danger or sword?...No, in all these things we are more than conquerors through him who loved us. For I am convinced that neither death nor life, neither angels nor demons, neither the present nor the future, nor any powers, neither height nor depth, nor anything else in all creation, will be able to separate us from the love of God that is in Christ Jesus our Lord." (Romans 8:35, 37-39, NIV)

That includes our own sin and failures. We must continue to bathe ourselves in God's Word. It is His Word that will combat the lies and set us free in God's truth!

So He said to the Jews who had believed Him, *"If you continue in My word*, you are truly My disciples. (Romans 8:31-32, BRB, emphasis mine)

What else must we do? We also must be sober-minded. I appreciate the humble response of two different people I had told about my past affair which were, in essence, "We are all just one choice away from doing the same thing." And they are right. On the other end of the spectrum are people like I had been who would declare, "I would never do such a thing!"

As Proverbs 16:18 says, "Pride goes before destruction, a haughty spirit before a fall." (NIV)

Consider Oswald Chambers' thoughts in *My Utmost for His Highest,*

If the Spirit of God has ever given you a vision of what you are apart from the grace of God, then you know that in reality there is no criminal half as bad as yourself could be without His grace. My 'grace' has been opened by God and 'I know that in me (that is, in my flesh) nothing good dwells' (Romans, 7:18). God's Spirit continually reveals to His children what human nature is like apart from grace.[17]

Part of winning the battle is to think soberly and reject Satan's lie that you are above anything.

For by the grace given to me I say to everyone among you not to think of himself more highly than he ought to think, but to think with sober judgment, each according to the measure of faith that God has assigned. (Romans 12:3, ESV)

Whose voice you choose to listen to in this life will make or break you. It will either hinder you from experiencing the fullness of a relationship with Christ or, if you choose to listen to God's voice alone, it can usher you into the most beautiful, intimate, loving relationship – one beyond your wildest imagination.

One of my favorite books that highlights this idea is a children's book by Max Lucado called, *You Are Special.*

Here is the short version of this sweet allegory. There is a group of small, wooden people called the Wemmicks, carved by their maker, Eli. The Wemmicks have boxes of gold stars and gray dot stickers they put on other Wemmicks. Someone might give you a gold star if you were pretty or had great talent. If you weren't very attractive, clumsy, or didn't have a unique talent, you would be given a gray dot. By the end of a day, a Wemmick would be covered with the praise or disapproval of their fellow Wemmicks in the form of gold stars and gray dots.

However, one Wemmick, Lucia, has no dots or stars. Other Wemmicks gave her gold stars and gray dots, yet all the stickers fell off. When the main character, Punchinello, asks her how she has no stickers, she replies, "It's easy. Every day I go visit Eli, the woodcarver."

So, Punchinello visits Eli to ask him why the stickers don't stick to Lucia:

The maker spoke softly. "Because she has decided that what I think is more important than what others think. The stickers only stick if you let them."

"What?"

"The stickers only stick if they matter to you. The more you trust my love, the less you care about the stickers."

"I'm not sure I understand."

Eli smiled. "You will, but it will take some time. For now, come and see me every day and let me remind you how much I care.[18]

Eli reiterated to Punchinello that he is special because he made him, and all that mattered is what he thinks.

What if you rejected the enemy's lies and replaced them with God's truth? What about the lies others have told you that don't align with God's Word? What would life look like if you were to focus on the voice of the One who made you—who calls you His own and His beloved, who knows you intimately and delights in you, who knows the number of hairs on your head and moved heaven and Earth to create you and be with you?

You would see the stickers fall.

You would live in the freedom and joy you were created to live in.

You would have peace that passes all understanding.

You would know, in the deepest parts of your heart, your true identity in Christ.

You would be in awe of who Jesus is and fall to your knees in worship!

P.S. Do you need to remind yourself of God's truth? Download my *Twenty-eight Days of Who I Am in Christ* Biblical Affirmation Cards at www.fromlovertobeloved.com/28days !

Chapter 11

When Life Feels Super Crappy

Walking through the aftermath of my affair was the hardest thing Garrett and I had ever done. It wasn't easy is the understatement of all understatements. Some days there would be a reprieve, and we might even laugh together. But many more days were filled with heartache, sadness, and anger. In these moments of hardship and pain, it could be easy to focus solely on all the difficulties.

However, we learned when we encounter challenges, we must look up to God and cling to His promises!

Enter God lesson number three from my hike in Estes Park.

Now, it is important to note *why* I decided on this particular hike and the route I chose. We had several friends staying at the YMCA in Estes, and when I asked for recommendations on where to go, they suggested the hike to Moraine Park. They insisted it was a beautiful hike, and I trusted them since they had been there.

And as I shared before, I specifically chose the route that went by the livery because, in my mind at the time, I would experience some majestic horses running through nature and coming over to me, having some kind of special God moment together. However, what had not occurred to me was I would be taking the same path to Moraine Park as the horses when people go horseback riding.

Here is the non-spiritual lesson of this trip. The horses do not have their own bathroom they do their "business" in before they start down the trail. Lesson? Don't go the way of the horses.

I encountered piles upon piles of crap on this supposedly beautiful trek to Moraine Park. I could hardly take in the sights around me as I focused entirely on the ground below my feet to avoid the poop mines.

Yet, believe it or not, God used the crap to speak to me again. "Brenna, life is like this path. It is a journey where I have promised you beauty and abundant life at the end of the path. I have prepared a place for you. However, there will be a lot of crap along the way, and if you keep your head down and only focus on the crap, you will miss out on the beauty I have surrounded you with even now. You will miss out on what I have to show you. And, you will lose hope of the promises I have given you."

This was a beautiful analogy to me because, in the midst of the crap path I had taken to see Moraine Park, I would have just turned around and given up had I not held onto the hope there was something beautiful at the end. I just needed to have faith and trust.

And such is the same with the path of life. If we do not cling to hope in the promises of God or have the lens of an eternal perspective in the midst of the crap, we will give up.

> I would have despaired unless I had believed
> that I would see the goodness of the LORD
> In the land of the living. Wait for the LORD;
> Be strong and let your heart take courage;

Yes, wait for the LORD. (Psalm 27:13-14, NASB)

How often in life do we get consumed by the piles of crap and fail to look up? Don't get me wrong. We aren't supposed to just *ignore* the crap. It needs to be acknowledged and dealt with. As Solomon writes, there is a season for everything:

> To everything there is a season, and a time for every purpose under heaven: a time to be born and a time to die, a time to plant and a time to uproot, a time to kill and a time to heal, a time to break down and a time to build, a time to weep and a time to laugh, a time to mourn and a time to dance, a time to cast away stones and a time to gather stones together, a time to embrace and a time to refrain from embracing, a time to search and a time to count as lost, a time to keep and a time to discard, a time to tear and a time to mend, a time to be silent and a time to speak, a time to love and a time to hate, a time for

war and a time for peace. (Ecclesiastes 3:1-8,
NKJV)

There is a time for every season—a time to weep and
mourn, for sadness and heartbreak. We aren't just to grin
and bear it and put on a good "happy" Christian face. I had
to mourn the hurt of my past, and I had never done that.
It took me twenty-five years to finally grieve my parents'
divorce.

When I allowed myself to mourn all that was lost, there
were times I felt transported to my little girl self. I was able
to weep for her and have compassion for her. We must have
compassion for ourselves! Therapist Beverly Engel states,
"Compassion is the antidote to shame. Self-compassion
acts to neutralize the poison of shame and remove the
toxins created by shame."[19]

I felt Jesus with me the whole time, crying together with
me and comforting me in my sadness. God longs to comfort us in our sadness.

> You keep track of all my sorrows. You have
> collected all my tears in your bottle. You have
> recorded each one in your book. (Psalm 56:8,
> NLT)

How can we be comforted if we never allow ourselves to feel sadness and mourn? Jesus calls us "blessed" when we mourn.

> Blessed are those who mourn, for they will be comforted. (Matthew 5:4, NIV)

Remember our John Eldredge quote? "A wound that goes unacknowledged and unwept is a wound that cannot heal."[20] We must acknowledge our hurt and come to the Lord with our pain! He will not let our pain go to waste.

> Therefore we do not lose heart. Though outwardly we are wasting away, yet inwardly we are being renewed day by day. For our light and momentary troubles are achieving for us an eternal glory that far outweighs them all. So we fix our eyes not on what is seen, but on what is unseen, since what is seen is temporary, but what is unseen is eternal. (2 Corinthians 4:16-18, NIV)

Of course, when we are in the middle of affliction or suffering, nothing about it feels "light" or "momentary."

Oftentimes, we don't see an end in sight. It doesn't feel like a "season." Instead, it feels like forever.

Yet, in the grand scheme of all eternity, God is using this affliction, this suffering, to mold and shape us to prepare us for an "eternal weight of glory beyond all comparison." This is a reason we can look up and hope.

> Those who look to him are radiant; their faces are never covered with shame. (Psalm 34:5, NIV)

Scripture assures us God is with us. He promises to never leave us nor forsake us (Deuteronomy 31:6). He promises to work all things for our good for the glory of His name (Romans 8:28).

Yet, we hurt. We suffer. We feel broken. And we must mourn what was lost—lost dreams, lost health, lost relationships, lost jobs, lost loved ones. These moments feel like the valley of the shadow of death. Yet this is precisely where God meets us!

> Even though I walk through the valley of the shadow of death, I will fear no evil, for you are with me; your rod and your staff, they

> comfort me. You prepare a table before me
> in the presence of my enemies; you anoint
> my head with oil; my cup overflows. (Psalm
> 23:4-5, NKJV)

I can say without a doubt that my most intimate, beautiful times with the Lord have been in the shadow of the valley of death. They were not high up on the mountain top. They were in the seasons of deep suffering in the ashes, coming to the end of myself and entirely having to let go and rely on Him. God uses our pain and suffering to draw us close to Him.

> The righteous cry out, and the Lord hears
> them; he delivers them from all their trou-
> bles. The Lord is close to the brokenhearted
> and saves those who are crushed in spirit. The
> righteous person may have many troubles,
> but the Lord delivers him from them all; he
> protects all his bones, not one of them will be
> broken. (Psalm 34:17-20, NIV)

If you have read the book of Psalms at all, David models being desperately real before the Lord with his pain, suffering, and questioning, and at the same time, he claims God's promises, gives Him praise, and ultimately puts his hope and trust in the Lord. Hard and sad feelings are not mutually exclusive with the hope, joy, and peace we can only find in God. You can feel both.

Garrett went through a season of being real with the Lord, questioning Him as to how a loving God would allow me, his wife, to have an affair. He would go for walks and yell at Him and, at the same time, desperately cling to Him. Garrett was lamenting.

Perhaps you need to lament, friend. In his book *Dark Clouds, Deep Mercy*, Mark Vroegop, describes lament as "...a loud cry, a howl, or a passionate expression of grief. However, in the Bible, lament is more than sorrow or talking about sadness. It is more than walking through stages of grief. Lament is a prayer in pain that leads to trust."[21]

Friend, look up. Be honest with God. Lament. Pray to God in your pain. Deal with the crap that comes, but also cling to God's promises here and now and for your future in heaven. You must hold onto *hope*. It is hope in the Lord that will carry you through.

> No one who hopes in you will ever be put to shame...Show me your ways, O Lord, teach

me your paths, guide me in your truth and teach me, for you are God my Savior, and my hope is in you all day long. (Psalm 25:3-5, NIV)

Chapter 12

Is There Hope After an Affair?

So, is there hope after an affair? I wouldn't have written this book and shared my story if I didn't believe there was hope after having an affair! There is hope! Not just for the broken pieces to be put back together, but to be made stronger and even more beautiful than before.

There were definitely days in our healing journey when I struggled with having hope. And there were many more days when Garrett expressed utter hopelessness. With all the hurt and agony surrounding his heart, he simply felt that even if we reconciled, the rest of our lives would be forever clouded by grief and sadness. Yet, in these moments, God supernaturally gave me enough hope and faith for both of us. It was God that solidified an unwavering hope within me.

In that first week after my confession when I was in Italy with my mom, we visited the Colosseum and the Roman Forum ruins. I was most struck by the ruins, a place where there was once life, love, joy, and laughter. Now all that remained were faint remnants of the things that once were. There was no life there now. There was no family, no home, no joy, and no hope.

Standing in this place, a shell of something that once was, I couldn't help but feel the ruins represented my life. I had destroyed our lives. I had ruined the love and joy that once abided there. There was no longer comfort in the word "home." Everything was uncertain. Everything seemed dead.

My heart sank as we passed the lifeless walls as I reflected upon this analogy to my own life. I felt immense, overwhelming sadness - there are just no words to describe the depths of my regret and the agony I felt. My affair had annihilated any hope of a future with Garrett and wrecked his heart.

As I sat with the question, "Is there any hope, Lord?" I noticed a tiny, lone red poppy growing out of the dust and dirt, its face seeking the light that God gives. This beautiful flower was full of hope and life in the middle of this forgotten, lifeless place. And, just like the analogy of the ruins I had made of our lives, God was giving me a new analogy.

Yes, I had caused massive destruction and ruin, but beauty and life would break through the broken and barren ground. In that sweet little flower, God fostered an assurance within me that He can bring beauty out of disaster. He planted a tiny seed of hope for a bright future and joy once again, engraving that poppy upon my heart as a physical picture of God's hope.

In the book of Isaiah, we see this hope:

> ...and to provide for those who grieve in Zion – to bestow on them a crown of beauty instead of ashes, the oil of gladness instead of mourning and a garment of praise instead of a spirit of despair. They will be called oaks of righteousness, a planting of the Lord for the display of his splendor. (Isaiah 61:3, NIV)

As the week went on in Italy and the physical separation from Garrett weighed heavily upon my soul, I continued to need God's truth spoken to my broken heart.

Several days after that one little red poppy became God's symbol of hope, my mom and I visited Pompeii. The devastation was evident on a much larger scale in Pompeii, reminding me again of my feelings about the destruction and ruin I had caused in my own life and marriage.

As we neared the end of the city and rounded the last bend of the street, I could barely catch my breath at the surprise that awaited me. To my right laid a vast sea of hope with thousands and thousands of red poppies. They stretched beyond what my eyes could see. Here was God, in His tender and faithful ways, encouraging my heart again that He saw me, He was with me, and I could place my hope in Him.

So, is there hope after cheating? The resounding answer is YES! But here's the thing. Our hope is not in ourselves. Our hope is not in our spouse. We have a responsibility to do the work, and we must see true, deep repentance from the one who cheated to move toward reconciliation. However, our ultimate hope is in God Himself because of who He is. Author Timothy Keller says, "We may hear our heart say, 'It's hopeless!' but we should argue back."[22]

So, here are ten truths about God to help you argue back.

God is faithful.

> If we confess our sins, He is faithful and just to forgive us our sins and to cleanse us from all unrighteousness. (1 John 1:9, NKJV)

> If we are unfaithful, he remains faithful, for he cannot deny who he is. (2 Timothy 2:13, NLT)

> Be strong and courageous. Do not be afraid or terrified because of them, for the Lord your God goes with you; he will never leave you nor forsake you. (Deuteronomy 31:6, NIV)

God is for us!

> If God is for us, who can be against us? He who did not spare His own Son but gave Him up for us all, how will He not also, along

with Him, freely give us all things? (Romans 8:31-32, NKJV)

The LORD is on my side; I will not be afraid. What can man do to me (Psalm 118:6, ESV)

God strengthens us.

Do not fear, for I am with you; do not be afraid, for I am your God. I will strengthen you; I will surely help you; I will uphold you with My right hand of righteousness. (Isaiah 41:10, NLT)

...but those who hope in the LORD will renew their strength. They will soar on wings like eagles; they will run and not grow weary, they will walk and not be faint (Isaiah 40:31, NIV)

God carries our burdens.

Honor and thanks be to the Lord, Who carries our heavy loads day by day. He is the God who saves us. (Psalm 68:19, NLV)

Cast your burden on the Lord, and He shall sustain you; He shall never permit the righteous to be moved. (Psalm 55:22, ESV)

God is patient.

The Lord is not slow to fulfill his promise as some count slowness, but is patient toward you, not wishing that any should perish, but that all should reach repentance. (2 Peter 3:9, ESV)

God is good.

Oh give thanks to the LORD, for he is good, for his steadfast love endures forever! (Psalm 107:1, ESV)

See what great love the Father has lavished on us, that we should be called children of God! And that is what we are! (1 John 3:1a, NIV)

> If you... know how to give good gifts to your children, how much more will your Father in heaven give good gifts to those who ask him. (Matthew 7:11, NIV)

God is compassionate and merciful.

> As a father shows compassion to his children, so the LORD shows compassion to those who fear him. (Psalm 103:13, ESV)

> I remember my affliction and my wandering, the bitterness and the gall. I well remember them and my soul is downcast within me. Yet, this I call to mind and therefore I have hope: Because of the Lord's great love we are not consumed, for his compassions never fail. They are new every morning; great is your faithfulness. I say to myself, "The Lord is my portion, therefore I will wait for him." (Lamentations 3:19-24, NIV)

God is Redeemer.

...who redeems your life from the pit and crowns you with love and compassion... (Psalm 103:4, NIV)

But now, this is what the Lord says— he who created you, Jacob, he who formed you, Israel: "Do not fear, for I have redeemed you; I have summoned you by name; you are mine." (Isaiah 43:1, NIV)

God is our comforter.

When doubts filled my mind, your comfort gave me renewed hope and cheer. (Psalm 94:19, ESV)

Praise be to the God and Father of our Lord Jesus Christ, the Father of compassion and the God of all comfort, who comforts us in all our troubles, so that we can comfort those in any trouble with the comfort we ourselves receive from God. (2 Corinthians 1:3-4, NIV)

God's love never fails.

> Because your love is better than life, my lips will glorify you. (Psalm 63:3, NIV)

> "Though the mountains be shaken and the hills be removed, yet my unfailing love for you will not be shaken nor my covenant of peace be removed," says the Lord, who has compassion on you. (Isaiah 54:10, NIV)

> We wait in hope for the LORD; he is our help and our shield. In him our hearts rejoice, for we trust in his holy name. May your unfailing love be with us, LORD, even as we put our hope in you. (Psalm 33:20-22, NIV)

Our God is good, and He is the God of hope! And to help you keep these truths in your heart and mind, I created a free download of these sweet truths about God that bring hope! Download it at www.fromlovertobeloved.com/hope

Restoration and reconciliation of your relationship will take time, hard work, and complete dependence upon the Lord. As the days turned into months that turned into years, I longed for the day for Garrett to forgive me. Yet, I couldn't force or demand his forgiveness. It was truly his gift to give freely.

After many weary days and nights and so many tears, Garrett extended complete forgiveness to me about two and a half years after my confession. Now, that may seem like a long time to some people and not very long to others. However, I believe he was extending some level of forgiveness to me every day when he decided to wake up next to me and the reality of my sin. At this two-and-a-half-year point, he felt he was done asking questions and ready to let go.

However, forgiveness is not the same as trust. It is possible to forgive someone but not trust them. You cannot demand trust either, but it can be rebuilt over time by living your life in a trustworthy and transparent manner. It will take a great willingness to humble yourself to help rebuild that trust. As the saying goes, "Trust takes years to build, seconds to break, and forever to repair."

I had to mourn the precious gift of trust that was no longer extended to me. It was mine. I had it. Garrett freely gave it to me and was completely vulnerable in doing so. It was so beautiful, so precious, and childlike. I didn't understand the vastness of this gift or appreciate his trust's incredible value until it was gone. To give someone trust is to allow access to one's heart, believing the person you have extended trust to would treat it with the utmost care and do everything they can to protect and nurture it. But, I took advantage of that trust and abused it greatly. I trampled the heart of the one who freely gave me access to it.

I hated wondering if Garrett would forever have a question in the back of his mind. What a horrible thing for me to have done, to cause the one I love, the one who loves me, to constantly doubt, wonder, and fear. My heart broke over the pain I had caused, and I was willing to do whatever it took to rebuild that trust.

For several months after I started a new job, Garrett drove me to and from work. I rarely went anywhere by myself; if I did, I called Garrett before and after to tell him where I was and when I would be home.

If Garrett had to go out of town for ministry, I offered to stay at my parents' house so he knew where I was and that I wasn't running off with someone. We gave each other full access to emails, phones, social media accounts, etc. We did whatever we needed to in order to be transparent and build trust with one another again.

To some, that all may sound ridiculous. But keep in mind I had completely obliterated his trust in me. I had lied straight to his face for so many years, and he had no idea. So it wasn't unreasonable for me to go to great lengths to rebuild trust. As I had truly repented and lived in the light, I had nothing to hide. And if you have truly repented and are living in the light, you have nothing to hide either.

Another piece of our healing process was that Garrett still had to earn my trust in the realm of his struggle with pornography. With a lot of humility, consistency, transparency, and time, our trust in one another has been rebuilt and has continued to grow stronger over the years.

Several months after Garrett forgave me, on the three-year anniversary of my confession, we renewed our wedding vows, turning that day of sadness into a day of celebration. We certainly didn't navigate this difficult road perfectly, but we chose to do it with the One who is perfect, and that made all the difference.

We have faced many joys and trials in the years since then, but we now have an unshakable, firm foundation we are standing on to see us through. For "...we know that God causes everything to work together for the good of those who love God and are called according to his purpose for them." (Romans 8:28, NLT)

Just like scripture says, God longs to work all things for your good and for His purpose, too! And please know if you are in the thick of the excruciating pain of infidelity, you are not alone. But, you will only *not* be alone when you actually invite other people in and ask for help!

Chapter 13

Don't Do It Alone

I'm a bit of an introvert. As a result of constantly attending new schools while growing up, I never established long-lasting friendships. Relationships are just plain hard for me. And as a young girl/woman, I didn't want to hang out with other girls. I wanted to play video games and sports. There weren't a lot of other girls doing either of those at the time.

Yet, as I have grown older and friendships have come and gone, I have realized just how precious faithful and true friends are. We must let others into our lives and do the work it takes to maintain deep friendships. We need people who see all of our mess and still stand with us despite our screw-ups. God intends for us to do this life with the help of community.

Curt Thompson, MD, author of *The Soul of Shame*, has this insight about community and healing, "The healing of shame takes place through the process of being known, through vulnerability in community."[23]

I had not allowed myself to be vulnerable in the context of community. As a result, I strayed far and wide from the path God had set before me. And He gave me a final lesson regarding community on that hike in Estes when I eventually arrived at Moraine Park.

Once I got there, I wasn't sure which direction to take to finish the loop to get me back to the YMCA. For some reason, I did not want to turn around and return the way I came. My little blue squiggly line map was worthless to a novice like me.

I wandered and wandered until I realized I should probably ask someone if they knew what direction I was heading in or where I should go. But, as God knows, I was deathly afraid of asking anyone for help or information, especially strangers. When I was younger and had to ask someone at the fast food restaurant to refill my soda, I couldn't even do that, no matter how much I wanted more.

God has shown me how these responses result from an overwhelming sense of shame in my life. After all, if I was just a pesky, dirty, annoying fly, as my grandmother had indicated, and I felt abandoned by both parents at different times, I was not valuable enough to bother anyone else. My shame had caused me to feel like a burden, and I could not ask for help or expect anyone to take the time to care about me. I still struggle to ask for help to this day! Yet, while on that trail, I had to ask someone because I just didn't know where to go.

God provided a lovely woman for me to approach whom I had passed a couple of times in my feeble attempt to figure out where I was. I gulped as I humbled myself and asked if she knew how to get back to the YMCA. She wasn't quite sure but got out her map which wasn't all that helpful either. We still weren't quite sure which direction I should go, so she walked alongside me to find more signs. Unfortunately, that didn't help either, so she walked back with me to her car, drove me back to the Y, and ensured I was safe. Interestingly enough, she had commented that she saw me earlier and thought to herself that it looked like I knew where I was going. What great masks we wear!

So often, we are too prideful, ashamed, hurt, or scared to ask for help. As a result, we remain lost, wandering in an unknown place, headed in the wrong direction. If only we had stopped to ask for help the first chance we got, how much wandering could be saved!

God used that experience to speak to me again: "Brenna, there will be times when you get off track, and you will get lost. But you have to ask for help. You have to have a community of people that can help keep you on the right path and point you toward me. You cannot do this alone."

In the past, I was on the right path in life, but I had taken a wrong turn, which led to another wrong turn, to another, and ended up somewhere very different from where God intended me to be.

Like scripture tells us, my disobedience is not uncommon. As it says in Isaiah 53:6, NLT, "All of us, like sheep, have strayed away. We have left God's paths to follow our own. Yet the Lord laid on him the sins of us all."

And even though we all have strayed and left God's paths, it says, "*yet* the Lord laid on him the sins of us all." *Yet.* Despite our rebellion, with full knowledge of our betrayal, and knowing we are prone to wander—*yet* the Lord laid on him the sins of us all.

> But he was pierced for our rebellion, crushed
> for our sins. He was beaten so we could

be whole. He was whipped so we could be
healed. (Isaiah 53:5, NLT)

He longs for us to be whole, and He paid the ultimate
price so we could heal. He helps us and guides us. He has
given us what we need to stay on the right path. After all,
we have God's Word to guide us, "Your word is a lamp for
my feet, a light on my path." (Psalm 119:105, NIV) But
it doesn't do us any good if we dismiss it or toss it in the
corner!

He also shows us the way. "Whether you turn to the
right or to the left, your ears will hear a voice behind you,
saying, 'This is the way, walk in it'" (Isaiah 30:21, NIV)

And God counsels us, "I will instruct you and teach you
in the way you should go; I will counsel you with my loving
eye on you." (Psalms 32:8, NIV)

———*ell*———

I don't know where you are on your journey. Maybe you
are dangerously close to starting an affair, have been engaging in an affair for some time (physical or emotional), or
have already confessed to an affair but haven't fully healed.
Perhaps you had a one-night stand and haven't confessed

it because it just happened once, and you try to pretend everything is okay.

Maybe there is still something, some experience, some lies you believe, holding you back from truly experiencing God for who He really is and from living the life of freedom and joy He created you to live in. Wherever you are, God is waiting to bathe you in His grace and to speak truth to your heart. There is hope for you!

I am living proof it is never too late to run back to God. It is never too late to discover who He really is and what He thinks about you. It is never too late to revisit the wounds of your past and allow healing to take place, to acknowledge them and weep over them.

And when you come running home, God does not stop to rub your nose in your sin or give you the cold shoulder. Instead, he runs out to meet you, He places a robe upon your shoulders and a ring upon your finger and says, "Welcome home, my precious child!" And He picks you up, dances with you, sings with delight over you, and throws a party because you are HIS BELOVED, and you are HOME.

URGENT PLEA!

If you have found this book helpful in any way, or believe it can be a help to others, please take two minutes to leave a review on Amazon so others can discover this book when they need it most. Here's a link to make it super easy!

www.fromlovertobeloved.com/review

THANK YOU SO MUCH!

Seven Days to F.E.E.L.

S till want to go deeper? There are so many excellent re-
sources and exercises that I learned during my healing
journey that I simply couldn't fit every single one into this
book. So, I created an additional resource, the *Seven Days
to F.E.E.L. Workbook,* to help you in your journey toward
living life in the fullness of Christ.

*I'm offering it to you for just $7 ($20 in savings)!
Get it now at www.tinyurl.com/sevendaystofeel!!*

This PDF workbook covers:
- Feelings

- Emotional Needs

- Experiences and how they affect our beliefs

- Lies we believe and combatting them with God's truth

Here is what we'll cover:

- Day 1 – God created you with Emotional Needs.

- Day 2 – Feelings? What Feelings? Learning to identify feelings.

- Day 3 – Why you need to express feelings.

- Day 4 – Practice identifying feelings.

- Day 5 – How your experiences impact your core beliefs/Core Belief Cycle (exercise) and ABC Theory exercise (honing in on individual events, how those events shaped a belief(s) and moving into a new truth/feeling).

- Day 6 – Identifying your heartfelt view of God.

- Day 7 – Replacing lies with God's truth (includes my *28 Days of Who I Am in Christ* Affirmation

Cards).

For just a dollar a day for a week, kick-start your reflective

healing journey together with God!

Visit www.tinyurl.com/sevendaystofeel!

SAMPLING OF CONTENT

Thank you for reading my book!

Other than my family, nothing brings me greater joy than to hear how God has moved in people's lives. I would love to hear from you!

Shoot me an email at brenna@skippinglikeacalf.com or follow and DM me on Instagram @brennanaufel.

End Notes

1. Eldredge, John and Stasi Eldredge. *Captivating* (Thomas Nelson, Inc, 2005).

2. Chambers, Oswald. *My Utmost for His Highest* (Grand Rapids, Michigan, Discovery House Publishers, 1992).

3. Chambers, Oswald. *My Utmost for His Highest.*

4. Piper, John. "How Can Couples Heal After Adultery?" Desiring God: Ask Pastor John. February 28, 2020. Podcast, episode 1440. https://www.desiringgod.org/interviews/how-can-couples-heal-after-adultery

5.

Piper, John. "How Can Couples Heal After Adultery?"

6. Beall, Cindy. *Healing Your Marriage When Trust Is Broken: Finding Forgiveness and Restoration.* (United States: Harvest House Publishers, 2011).

7. Lewis, C.S. *Yours, Jack.* Letter to Miss Breckenridge. (Harper Collins, 2008), p. 116.

8. Beverly Engel. "Healing Your Shame and Guilt Through Self Forgiveness" *The Compassion Chronicles – Psychology Today* (blog), June 1, 2 0 1 7 , https://www.psychologytoday.com/intl/blog/the-compassion-chronicles/201706/healing-your-shame-and-guilt-through-self-forgiveness

9. Eldredge, John. *Wild at Heart: Discovering the Secret of a Man's Soul* (Nashville, Tennessee, Thomas Nelson, 2001), p. 108.

10. Pascal, Blaise and Molinier, Auguste. *The Thoughts of Blaise Pascal* (London, Chiswick Press, 1905).

11.

Van der Kolk, Bessel A. *The Body Keeps a Score: Brain, Mind, and Body in the Healing of Trauma.* (New York, New York, Penguin Publishing, 2015).

12. Seamands, David A. *Healing of Memories.* (United States: David C. Cook, 1985).

13. Carmichael, Amy, David Hazard. *I Come Quietly to Meet You: An Intimate Journey in God's Presence.* (United States: Baker Publishing Group, 2005), p. 66.

14. Sledge, Tim. *Making Peace with Your Past: Help for Adult Children of Dysfunctional Families.* (United States: LifeWay Press, 1991).

15. Thompson, Curt. *The Soul of Shame: Retelling the Stories We Believe About Ourselves.* (United States: InterVarsity Press, 2015).

16. Beverly Engel. "Healing Your Shame and Guilt Through Self Forgiveness" *The Compassion Chronicles – Psychology Today* (blog), June 1, 2017, accessed September 26, 2022, https://www.psychologytoday.com/intl/blog/th

e-compassion-chronicles/201706/healing-your-s
hame-and-guilt-through-self-forgiveness

17. Chambers, Oswald. *My Utmost for His Highest.*

18. Lucado, Max. *You are Special*. (United States: Scholastic, 1997).

19. Beverly Engel. "How to Forgive Yourself for Becoming a Victim of Emotional Abuse*" The Compassion Chronicles – Psychology Today* (blog), March 26, 2022, accessed September 26, 2022, https://www.psychologytoday.com/us/blog/the -compassion-chronicles/202203/how-forgive-yo urself-becoming-victim-emotional-abuse

20. Eldredge, John. *Wild at Heart: Discovering the Secret of a Man's Soul.*

21. Vroegop, Mark. *Dark Clouds, Deep Mercy: Discovering the Grace of Lament.* (United States: Crossway, 2019).

22. Keller, Timothy. *Walking with God Through Pain and Suffering*. (United States: Penguin Publishing Group, 2013).

23. "Curt Thompson – at Denver Seminary – Therapeutic Techniques to Work through Shame." Vimeo video, 43.21 minutes, posted by "Denver Institute," September 16, 2016 https://vimeo.com/198258058

www.ingramcontent.com/pod-product-compliance
Lightning Source LLC
La Vergne TN
LVHW051556080426
835510LV00020B/3008